W9-CLO-140

DIAMOND RIVER

918.7
Gar

90144

Garavini di Turno.
Diamond River.

Date Due

The Library
Nazareth College of Rochester, N. Y.

PRINTED IN U.S.A.

DIAMOND RIVER

◆

SADIO GARAVINI DI TURNO

Translated from the Italian by Peter Green

A HELEN AND KURT WOLFF BOOK

HARCOURT, BRACE & WORLD, INC.

NEW YORK

DISCARDED

NAZARETH COLLEGE LIBRARY

90144

© 1962 by Casa Editrice Valentino Bompiani
English translation © 1963 by Hamish Hamilton Ltd. and
Harcourt, Brace & World, Inc.

All rights reserved. No part of this book may be
reproduced in any form or by any mechanical means,
including mimeograph and tape recorder, without
permission in writing from the publisher.
First American edition

Originally published in Italy
under the title *Lolomai*

All facts and incidents narrated here are true and authentic; in some
cases, however, the names and characteristics of people
have been changed to protect their privacy.

Library of Congress Catalog Card Number: 63-8082
Printed in the United States of America

918.7
Grar

Contents

Contents

Chapter 1

◆

A PROSPECT OF DIAMONDS

My horse, without warning, side-stepped, jerking me back to reality. I had dug my heels into his flanks but had then failed to put him to a gallop, and this omission he clearly found confusing. So I began to think out loud, partly to ease my own misery, partly to calm my nervous mount.

"Our *finca*'s had it, old boy," I told the horse. "The hurricane destroyed everything. Including our farm. Take a look at the fields—see what they've been reduced to. Nothing's left of our two years' hard work but a sea of mud."

The horse jogged along, head hanging low, at the same lazy trot as before.

But it was true; the hurricane had swept away all my hopes, all the fruits of my toil—stables, herds, crops, farm implements, the two years of my life that I had spent here in Venezuela. Two years ago, on the advice of a friend in Caracas, I had purchased this *finca*, a four-thousand-acre estate set in the foothills of the Andes at Bocono, a township in the Trujillo *estado*. I had worked my guts out on that ranch, stripping off the timber for plowing, building farmhouse and outbuildings and stables, damming streams to irrigate the fields, breaking up acres of rich virgin soil.

On the strength of a loan from the Banco Agricolo y Pecuario I had purchased tractors and mechanical plows. As soon as the land was ready I sowed three hundred bushels of seed potatoes. The crop promised to be an exceptionally good one. So without looking very far into the future (rather like the hermit in the old story, who sat dreaming of what he might have bought with the proceeds from the honey he never sold) I felt well satisfied all round—with myself, with the work I had accomplished, with the excellent prospects ahead of me. My initial success encouraged me in the belief that I had a real vocation for farming.

There was a small stream that ran across my land, in which I took a refreshing dip at sundown every evening. The torrential rains that accompanied the hurricane transformed this stream into a raging torrent. Its waters rose and overflowed their banks, breaching the dike that protected my arable land, flooding across the entire ranch. In a few hours the fields were swamped, the peons' huts carried away, all my young trees uprooted. When the water subsided the land looked as though it had been blasted by lightning: a wilderness of stinking mud strewn with tree trunks and the swollen carcasses of dead cattle. All that remained of my bright hopes now was a waste of yellow mire, streaked with huge gray and purplish patches, which soon baked hard in the sun, forming a solid crust. Long irregular cracks then appeared, crosshatching the crust into a series of irregular-shaped blocks, beneath which my labor and my hopes lay buried forever.

In Venezuela both the rainy and the dry seasons are equally oppressive. I was well aware that when you emigrate to a distant country you have got to be prepared for anything: to forget all your old habits and assumptions, and accept the fact that good intentions alone are not enough to overcome the challenge of climatic extremes. But despite this, I had really come to the end of my tether. At that moment I felt utterly drained, incapable of starting over again, and infected with a chronic terror of the tropics, as all-pervasive as it was ineradicable. Determined to cut loose from this whole venture as fast as I could, I sold the *finca*. When all my outstanding debts had been cleared, I was left with only a few thousand bolivars to my name. I cashed the lot, and set out for the capital.

❖   ❖   ❖

The bolivar, worth about 30 U. S. cents, is one of the hardest currencies in the world, but Caracas is one of the most expensive cities in the world, too. Oil was struck there less than forty years ago, on the eastern side of Lake Maracaibo; and ever since then the wells at Los Borrosos have poured a non-stop flood of capital into Venezuela. Caracas has not changed much in those forty years; it was, and still is, a sort of permanent camp, especially the modern residential area stretching down the Rio Guaira valley. The hills on one side sprout a sort of multicolored leprous rash—the tin-roofed wooden shacks known as *ranchitos*; opposite them soars a fungoid growth of white cubist-style skyscrapers.

The old-time colonial city, with its single-storied houses and Spanish wrought-iron window gratings, has practically vanished altogether, though traces of it are still to be found in certain picturesque back streets, well away from the center. Today, however, even these are in danger of destruction: the building mania of the *Caraqueños* lets nothing stand in its way. They are determined to turn their capital into a model of modern architectural planning, and have drawn up a gigantic master-design that amply reflects the richness of their material resources.

Nevertheless, there are still some remote regions upcountry where, even today, strangers who venture into Indian territory are liable to get poisoned arrows shot at them; relatively few of the tribesmen have ever had any contact with Europeans. In the Maracaibo area, indeed, the Motilones regard the white man as their most deadly enemy, and wage relentless war upon him.

I had no very clear idea where I was going. After drifting around the city for a while I finally ended up in the Don Luis Bar. Here I hoped to cool off and rest for a while: the normal temperature of Caracas was ninety-five degrees in the shade, with a corresponding degree of humidity. No sooner had I sat down, however, than a voice exclaimed: *"Que tal, hace mucho tiempo que no te veo, amigo!*—It's a long time since I've seen you, my friend." It was Felix Cardona, the friend who had suggested my buying the *finca* two years previously. There he sat, a little farther down the same bench, with the air of one who has recently concluded a profitable pact with the Devil. Cardona was Spanish by birth (or, to be more precise, a Catalan), a brave, liberal-minded fellow bursting with energy and vitality: he struck me as a typical example of the pioneering mentality, one of Nature's explorers.

I stared at him for a moment in astonishment. Meeting him now, so soon after the disaster that had befallen my venture, gave me a strange feeling that I was keeping an appointment with destiny. Cardona was slightly shorter than average, his features lined (yet by no means coarse), his skin deeply tanned by the tropical sun. There was something about him that inspired immediate confidence. In any case, I felt so desperately miserable just then that I would have unburdened myself to anyone, no matter who.

He sat and listened to the full story of the disaster. His face gave nothing away.

"Well," he said at length, "and what do you plan to do now?"

"I'm not staying here, whatever happens," I said. "I've been away from city life too long. I couldn't get used to all this noise and bustle again."

By now we were on our fourth round of whiskies, and I ordered a fifth.

"Listen," Cardona said, after a while, "you're still a young man. In fact, you may well be the only person capable of taking on a little job I've got at the back of my mind. I'm getting on, you know; beginning to feel my age a bit. Not so keen on travel as I used to be."

He paused again, and I realized that he was talking in earnest.

For the past thirty years he had been in the service of the Venezuelan government, and his official duties had taken him through the length and breadth of the country, into hitherto unexplored areas. I knew, too, that he had spent considerable periods living in close contact with tribes who had never set eyes on a white man prior to his arrival. There was no doubt about it, Felix Cardona had seen more of Venezuela, and the upper reaches of the Amazon across the border in Brazil, than any traveler now alive. That he began to feel weary of it all did not surprise me in the least. He had probably put by enough to retire: I visualized him leading a peaceful existence somewhere on the coast of his beloved Catalonia. But the forest does not let a man go quite so easily once it has got a grip on him, as I found out for myself.

When he resumed talking, he told me of the expedition from which he had just returned; he had journeyed right to the Brazilian border, his task being to determine the precise line of the frontier.

"One of the Indians working for me," he said, "was the headman of the Taurepán tribe. These Indians are of Carib stock, and live on both sides of the frontier. We got our surveying job done in about six months. After it was finished my Brazilian colleagues made tracks south, and I went back with Mundo—that was the headman's name—to have a look at his tribe. Spent a week there with them. Somewhere in the district where the Taurepán are settled there's a river chock-full of diamonds."

He paused to let the idea sink in.

"You can imagine what'd happen if the news got around," he murmured. (The bar was empty apart from the two of us.) "Why don't you have a shot at it? It's not an easy proposition, but you've got Mundo there; I taught him enough Spanish for him to understand simple statements, and to make himself understood in return."

I had already made up my mind, and was only afraid that he might be discouraged by the faint note of perplexity I knew must have crept into my voice. So I hastily told him that I found the scheme interesting—very interesting indeed. Especially since it presented a fair prospect of success.

"For a courageous man," Cardona assured me, "it offers endless possibilities."

"What's the river called?"

"It hasn't a name yet. You won't find it on any map, either. The Indians call it Liparú. I've christened it the Rio Blanco. It rises in Brazil and is a tributary of the Uai-parú."

"There's one snag," I told Cardona. "I know absolutely nothing about diamonds."

"That's the least of your worries. I can tell you quite a bit. Everyone's a learner here, one way or another."

Cardona's silences were legendary; and it did you no good to try to force him to talk against his will. However, after a while either the thought of the diamonds or the whisky he had drunk loosened his tongue again, and he told me a great deal more about the Taurepán tribe and their primitive Eden. Then he said: "Come and have a bite with me. I'll show you the diamonds I found. I made a sketch-map of the area, too."

Chapter 2

◆

PRELIMINARY SKIRMISHES

During the week that followed I learned a few basic phrases of Taurepán dialect; got a minimal working knowledge of the techniques employed for finding, sieving, and classifying diamonds; and committed to memory the route that Cardona had marked out on his sketch-map. He also furnished me with two photographs that I could show the Indians in lieu of a letter of introduction. One of these showed Mundo alone, and the other was of Mundo and Cardona standing side by side.

The first leg of my journey would take me to Ciudad Bolívar, and presented no particular difficulties. My troubles were liable to begin afterward, and to increase the farther south I went. I would have to make for the upper reaches of the Caroní, a river that lay on the far side of the Gran Sabana, and beyond which began the endless forest that covers the entire region about the Amazon. My last contact with remotely civilized human beings would be at Uriman, a village that consisted of a small cluster of huts on the outskirts of the forest. Uriman was a completely isolated outpost, and might prove difficult of access to a traveler loaded with bulky but indispensable equipment—tools, arms, provisions, and the like.

Once the decision to mount an expedition had been made, I lost no time in getting down to details. During the week I had spent in Cardona's company I discovered that a man called Vaughan had a small private aircraft that he flew between Ciudad Bolívar and Uriman throughout the dry season, ferrying both passengers and freight. He touched down halfway at a site that he had cleared himself (with a view to developing it for tourists) and had christened Canaima. My best plan was to go and find Vaughan on his home ground, so to speak. I therefore said good-by to Cardona and flew down to Ciudad Bolívar, where I would be able to procure all the equipment and provisions I needed. Scarcely had I landed, however, before I was told that Vaughan had left for Canaima the previous afternoon, and would not be back for another two or three days.

I took advantage of the delay to stock up with basic provisions: flour, rice, bacon, coffee, sugar, and salt. I also purchased arms and tools: a repeating rifle, boxes of ammunition, a big sheath knife, several machetes, a waterproof *chinchorro* or hammock; a *suruca*, which consists of three superimposed sieves used by prospectors—the first sieve catches diamonds of three carats and more, the second those of one carat or more, while the third sifts the muddy residue; *pale*, or special rounded shovels, octagonal iron crowbars, pointed at both ends; a heavy hammer, fishing tackle, medical supplies, a compass, and heaven knows what else.

Two days later Vaughan arrived, on the dot. The moment I saw him I had a definite feeling that we had met somewhere before. A moment's searching in my memory and I had it. He was one of the American fighter aces that I had met, briefly, during the war and whose picture I had seen a number of times in various papers and magazines. Either because he could not quite place me, or else by reason of that natural taciturnity which some Americans have in common with the English (I have never quite managed to accustom myself to it), Charles Vaughan did not exactly welcome me with open arms. I got straight to the point and told him how I needed to hire his plane. Persuading him was a far from easy business.

"What are you after down there?" he inquired.

"I've been sent out by a paper to write the place up."

"It's dangerous. Mighty dangerous. You got any idea what it's like?"

I mumbled vaguely, still hopeful.

"You could even get yourself done in there."

"I can't help that," I said, "I've got to make the trip." I was by no means sure of prevailing over his distrustful attitude.

"Not a hope of landing at Uriman just now, anyway. The strip hasn't dried out yet."

I told him a few days would make no odds. In the end he capitulated.

"O.K. If you're dead set on going we'll hop down there in a few days. I got to go back to Canaima right now, but I'll be back Sunday. Get you to Uriman Monday. That do you?"

The first step had been successfully negotiated. I felt nothing could stop me now. I wired Cardona the date of my departure, and sat down to wait. On Sunday evening I had dinner with Vaughan in a little restaurant on the bank of the Orinoco. It was plain that he had something on his mind. "Look," he said, "just between friends, do you mind telling me why you're here? The real reason, I mean."

"To write articles for a national paper."

"Occurs to me," Vaughan said, "that I wouldn't mind stringing along with you, at that."

This was an unlooked-for complication, and one not at all to my liking. I had made up my mind to travel solo, and in any case Charles Vaughan was not the companion I would have chosen had I been looking for a partner. I objected that the canoe I would be using during the first part of the trek was not big enough to accommodate two passengers.

"I wasn't thinking of canoes," the American said. "The only way I travel is by plane. There just might be room to land somewhere in the forest, see? Suppose you got the Indians friendly, you know what you ought to do? Look around for a biggish clearing, have them chop down a few trees, and that's it. I only need a strip three hundred yards long. Then send one of the Indians back with a message that the job's been done."

"Sure," I said. "I'll think it over."

In these parts you find more people with something to hide

than you tend to run across elsewhere. But Vaughan didn't look the sort who had a murder on his conscience. He just looked at you and said nothing. No one was going to take *him* for a ride if he could help it.

"You got any idea the head start it'll give you, having a plane around? Fly in any supplies you need. Get your articles back to your paper in no time."

He didn't believe me, and he was making no attempt to conceal the fact. It was out of character for him to talk so freely.

"I get the point," I said. "We'll see how things go, shall we?"

"Fair enough." He held out his hand. "We'll meet again the day after tomorrow, at the airport. Six o'clock."

The following afternoon Cardona turned up.

"Got your wire all right," he told me. "Decided I might as well come with you as far as Uriman. I want to make sure those Indians let you have my canoe."

I told him something of my conversation with Vaughan, and he agreed that I was right to distrust the man. If the real object of the expedition leaked out, I would have a whole swarm of adventurers on my tail. I showed him the equipment I had bought. The only items missing were a waterproof bag (which could also, at a pinch, be used as a life belt) and some canned meat and sardines.

"The Indians," Cardona told me, "have an absolute passion for sardines, so don't hand them out too freely. Keep them for special occasions."

Next morning we all three turned up at the airport, bright and early. When Cardona appeared Vaughan was clearly put out and, characteristically, made no attempt to conceal the fact.

"Well, where are *you* off to?" he asked him, scowling.

"He's coming to Uriman with me," I said.

"Can't be done. The plane won't take three of us *and* all this gear; much too heavy."

"Very well, then," I said, "we'll make two trips. I'll pay you double."

He argued a bit longer, so as not to lose face, but finally agreed to make a second trip with the equipment.

An hour and a half after take-off we were flying over Canaima, the outpost that Vaughan himself had created. It was quite near the Carrao Falls, and as we came in we could see them gleaming white in the sunlight. Just above the settlement the river widened out into a broad palm-fringed lagoon: the trees were the *Mauritia flexuosa*, known locally as *moriches*. On one bank there stood a large bungalow, complete with restaurant and bar. Proudly Vaughan enumerated the various comforts which his "hotel" had to offer.

"Rooms with private baths," he shouted, his voice struggling against the plane's rackety old engine. "Running water everywhere, best and purest water in the world, straight from the Carrao Falls—"

"All the same you're on the wrong tack," Cardona shouted. "Making the Indians go around naked to give American tourists a kick—that's all wrong, for a start."

Vaughan swore coarsely. "Balls," he said, "the Indians are the way nature made 'em. No one's going to teach *them* to wear collars and ties, not even the Karamata missionaries. Anyway, I'm telling you, Canaima's going to become a world-famous tourist center—"

Cardona laughed this idea to scorn, but I kept quiet, judging it wise not to irritate our pilot any further. We passed over Karamata, site of the Spanish Catholic mission, and shortly afterward saw the melancholy mass of Mt. Auyán-Tepuy rising above the horizon. Cardona had been the first man to scale this peak. Then there unfolded beneath us the vast (and vastly impressive) expanse of the Gran Sabana, with the Caroní River winding its way across it.

"*Está podrido de diamantes!*" Cardona muttered to me. "The whole area's lousy with diamonds. But it guards them well. Possibly no one will ever succeed in finding all of them. Now and then some lucky prospector manages to pierce the outer crust of *moco de hierro* that lies above the rock formations where diamonds are deposited, and maybe he digs out a small stone or two. But the returns don't justify the expense, and the whole undertaking's far too dangerous."

After three hours' flying we sighted Uriman. The landing strip was in a very bad condition, potholed, puddle-strewn, and covered with long grass. We made a couple of dummy runs to survey it. Finally, with a display of skill that did much to compensate for the less pleasant aspects of his character, Vaughan spotted his best line of approach, made a beautiful three-point landing, and taxied to a stop just on the outskirts of the village.

We were met by a bizarre-looking collection of people, who hurried out toward the plane. There were about twenty of them: bearded Europeans, Indians, Negroes, and every imaginable product of the three races in combination. Some of them wore ragged trousers, others were naked except for a pair of pants or an exiguous loincloth. The most elaborately attired, a group of Indians who sported hats and boots, looked like so many scarecrows. They all knew Cardona, and each of them had some question to ask him.

Vaughan lugged out his thermos and poured himself a cup of coffee. Then he stretched himself, strolled back to the strip, and clambered aboard again. "See you tomorrow," he called, and slid the cockpit cover shut.

Cardona informed everybody, with a great show of conviction, that I was a real journalist. At once they all gathered around me to unburden their personal problems and grievances—all, that is, except the Indians, who were apparently satisfied with the conditions in which they lived. They were Camaragoto tribesmen, of Carib stock.

We could not refuse the coffee pressed upon us, with positively Levantine insistence, by a character known as Barabbas, who (so Cardona told me) had been lucky enough, some years back, to find a 170-carat diamond. But being an ignorant, simple sort of fellow, he had sold it for 300,000 bolivars. In three months he had spent the lot and had come back from Caracas with his tail between his legs, though absolutely convinced that he was destined to find more diamonds of similar quality.

From where we were we could see the beginning of the forest, which spread its dense and tangled mass over hundreds of thousands of square miles of territory: eastward it stretched as far as British Guiana, and toward the south it reached beyond the Brazilian frontier to embrace the entire Amazon basin. A large proportion of this "Green Hell" had never been explored.

A couple of hours' walking brought us into the outskirts of this jungle. Here the heat was not so intense: the sun could scarcely filter through the dense foliage overhead. Suddenly a pack of mangy dogs came bounding out to meet us, furiously barking. We had reached our destination. The women, who had been busy at work on the threshing floor, disappeared inside their huts. Once they had recognized Cardona, the men called off their dogs. Someone went to find Francisco, their headman.

The village was not far from the river; we could hear the murmur of water somewhere close at hand. The huts were strung out around an open square. An old woman sat in one corner busily searching for lice in the hair of a small and unspeakably filthy infant. Whenever she caught one she popped it into her mouth. Some of the other women went back to the piles of manioc roots they had abandoned when we showed up, and began to pound away at them again. (These Indians call manioc *yuca*. The root contains a poisonous liquid that has to be extracted to make the manioc edible. The pounded pulp is used as the basic ingredient of *casabe*, the staple local variant of the tortilla, a large, thin, flat griddle-cake.) All of them were swathed in the most appalling tattered rags.

By now Francisco had been found and summoned. He was a man in his forties, tall and powerfully built, his scalp close-shaven apart from a curious quiff on the crown.

Cardona came straight to the point. "This is a friend of mine," he said. "He has got to get to Taurepán country. He will have to travel up the Caroní, the Icaparú, and the Hacha as far as it is navigable. He needs my canoe, and four men to go with him. I know you for a brave warrior, and I would be very pleased if you were to be one of them. In return, when I go back to Caracas, I will speak well of you to the Great White Chief."

By this Cardona meant the Venezuelan Ministry of Agriculture and Forestry, which from time to time, through his intercession, made an issue of shirts and trousers for the Indians.

According to Cardona's sketch-map, it ought to be possible to travel by canoe all the way to the Rio Blanco. But the journey was bound to be both lengthy and difficult, since during the dry season certain stretches became unnavigable. On top of this Francisco and his companions were Camaragoto tribesmen, with a veneer of civilization about them: they went in fear of the Taurepán, and would not go anywhere near them if they could avoid it.

Cardona turned back to Francisco. "The outward journey will take ten to twelve days," he said. "The return downstream not more than four or five. Tell me how much you want for this."

Francisco conferred for a moment with his fellow tribesmen.

"Taurepán Indian braves have poisoned arrows," he said. "My men will not go to Rio Blanco."

They agreed to escort me as far as the Hacha River, but no farther. In return they demanded twenty yards of red cloth, thirty tins of meat, thirty tins of sardines, ten large fishhooks, and a roll of *casabe*.

"So far so good," Cardona told me. "With any luck you'll be able to persuade them to accompany you a bit farther when you reach the Hacha."

Then, without waiting to see whether I agreed or not, he said to Francisco: "Very well. My friend accepts your conditions. There's just one thing, though: we haven't got any red cloth. What would you like instead?"

Francisco retired once more to confer with his friends. They decided that the position could be adjusted by asking for fifty tins of meat and sardines instead of thirty.

"Done," said Cardona. "Now let's go and inspect the *curiara*"—the local term for pirogue, or canoe—"I want to see what sort of condition it's in."

We found it by the riverbank, hidden away under a layer of branches, and pushed it into the water. It was a handy little craft, fashioned by burning out from a single tree trunk, in excellent trim and well able to take a load of up to half a ton.

The following day the Indians were at Uriman shortly before Vaughan touched down. I checked the gear: all present and correct. I embraced Cardona, and the emotional stress of this farewell scene affected me so much that I actually embraced Vaughan, too. As the aircraft bore them away I stood there, waving frantically, till they were out of sight. Then the Indians transported my equipment and provisions to the village. I decided to sleep out in the open, wrapped in my *chinchorro*: this seemed preferable to the stench and filth of the huts. All around me flickered the watch fires, lit mainly to keep mosquitoes at bay. Next day my adventure would begin in earnest.

Chapter 3

◆

THE JOURNEY UPRIVER

We were up at dawn. While the Indians busied themselves with getting the canoe ready, I brewed coffee for all of us. We were seen off from the riverbank by the entire village, dogs included. Antonio and José paddled from the bow, Francisco and Angelito in the stern, while I sat amidships, with the gear and provisions.

Francisco's companions were lithe, intelligent-looking men, each of whom had an almost uncanny knack of anticipating or divining his companions' precise needs in advance. Every separate maneuver was conducted by all three: they had a system of wordless co-operation. Even when one of them deemed his assistance unnecessary for some particular task, he nevertheless followed every movement the other two made, with the closest possible attention.

We steered right across the river, making for the shelter of the left-hand bank, which offered us some protection from the full strength of the current. Even so there were moments when it looked as though our little craft might not make it. On such occasions Francisco would steer still closer in to the shore, while the two men up at the prow laid hold of the branches protruding from the water and, by main force, kept us clear of the deep, eddying currents out in midstream. The canoe, loaded down as it was with all my equipment and stores, rode only a few bare inches above water level.

The accuracy with which the four Indians determined their

stint at the paddle, turn and turn about, was a source of never-ending astonishment to me. I checked them against my wrist watch. Every twenty minutes, to the second, two of them—one at the prow and one at the stern—would stop paddling, without a word or sign having been exchanged between them. They would simultaneously put down their *canaletes* (as the paddles were called), spit the tobacco they had been chewing over the side, take several deep breaths, drink a little water, rinse their faces—and then, twenty minutes later exactly, both start paddling again.

We progressed at an average speed of five or six miles an hour. The Caroní is a broad and majestic river; one of the most beautiful rivers, indeed, I have ever seen, its surface a vivid blue, with the forest—not to mention orchids of every color under the sun—reflected in it. The trees, too, displayed infinite variety of shape and hue: they overhung the water, roots embracing bare rock, branches intertwined. Lianas and other climbing plants wound themselves around the roots of trees such as the *yara-yara* (a member of the Annonaceae family, which attains a height of about twenty-five feet) and the *cumares* palm, a giant sixty-footer, twisting and turning upward around trunks and branches in endless spiral ascent. As we approached, the turtles and alligators that had been sunning themselves on the banks dived lazily into the water.

About eleven o'clock on the first day of the trip Francisco steered the canoe in toward a small rocky spit and beached it under the shade of a big *sarrapia* tree. (The *sarrapia* is used for medicinal purposes, and its seeds give off a pleasant aromatic scent.) The sun was blazing hot, and the Indians, stripping off their few ragged garments, plunged into the water for a dip. I followed their example without delay, and felt much refreshed as a result.

After our swim Francisco prepared the midday meal: one tin of sardines between Antonio and José, another for himself and Angelito, a third for me. With the sardines each of us had a slice of casabe. I found my portion so hard that I had to soak it a long while in water before I could even chew it. When I realized that a whole tin of sardines had been put aside for my exclusive use I ate two only, and presented the remainder to Francisco. He seemed to appreciate the gesture. This supplementary ration was divided equally between the four of them.

Soon we cast off and resumed our journey. The frequent loops and bends in the river meant endless turbulence; at times the current gave the impression that it was trying to thrust the dense jungle back from either bank. At the approach of human intruders birds of all shapes and colors flew up into the air, while big green yellow-headed parrots screeched in furious protest.

Our diet displayed the same sort of natural variety. When, about two in the afternoon, we tied the canoe up to a liana in order to have a short siesta, José slipped off into the jungle, taking with him bow, arrows, and machete. He returned with a bunch of wild pineapples, about the same size as oranges and very sweet-tasting. That evening we found something even better. We had landed on a small island that Francisco knew of; and while Antonio was fishing and José busy slinging our hammocks among the trees, Francisco and I went for a stroll along the sandy foreshore, ending up in the middle of the island, where a clump of palm trees formed a sort of cool oasis. We noticed fairly fresh animal tracks imprinted on the sand, and Francisco told me they were those of the turtle. This, he said, was the time of year when turtles laid their eggs.

Hour by hour, I felt, we were penetrating more deeply into a wholly alien world, compounded of alternating hopes and fears: a world, to my way of looking at it, not only foreign but actively hostile, and in which I was now immersed. I felt considerable gratitude to Francisco for his words of explanation.

To prevent their eggs going dry and leathery, the turtles choose a damp spot in which to lay them. Once they have picked their site, they scrape a hole some eighteen inches deep and put a layer of dry leaves at the bottom. Then they lay their eggs on the leaves, taking care that none of them touch each other. Finally they cover them up with sand, smoothing it out so carefully that the wild animals which habitually rob nests of their eggs scarcely ever succeed in unearthing a turtle's cache.

According to Francisco, the tracks we had seen were some days old, and it was not worth our while to follow them. But a little later we came upon another trail, and this time it was absolutely fresh. We followed it to the top of a sandy mound, and here the Indian at once located the position of the nest. He scooped up handfuls of sand till he was about a foot down, and there, sure enough, were the eggs: he looked very pleased with himself as he picked them out. We had a wonderful meal that evening: boiled rice, fried fish, turtle-egg omelettes, and wild pineapple.

When I awoke next morning there were wisps of gray mist hanging above the surface of the river, and a few stars still twinkled faintly in the sky. I lingered thus for a while, eyes open, listening to the slow lap and gurgle of the water, while Francisco made coffee.

That day we reached the first of the three sets of rapids we had to pass through on our journey. About midmorning I became aware of a distant roaring sound. Then, quite suddenly, the river widened out around a bend into a lagoon of crystal-clear water, with a band of scummy foam lying across its farther end—the point at which the river plunged from a height of some sixty feet, down ten or twelve rocky channels each apparently less than a yard wide.

Several dozen alligators that had been sunning themselves on the bank now slid into the water, one after another, and followed us at three or four yards' distance, their blank eyes fixed on the canoe. I had just picked up my rifle and was about to take a pot shot at them when Francisco stopped me.

"Leave them be," he said. "They could overturn us with one flick of their tail. A nasty death."

When we drew near the rapids they turned back. I learned later that these alligators never go up through the big river rapids.

We pulled in to the left-hand bank, and Francisco went ashore to take a look at the cataract, which presented few difficulties. Then we lashed two ropes to the bow thwart, and two more to the stern, each of us tying the free end of one rope around his waist. In this way we managed to haul the canoe through the rapids, though it was hard work getting it into the channel Francisco selected, which could not have been more than six feet wide, if that. Quite apart from the danger of piling up on the rocks, there was a constant threat that the force of the current would overturn the canoe at any moment.

This ordeal lasted some three hours. If we had relaxed for a moment we should have ended up as alligator-bait. But finally we got the canoe through into clear water again. Angelito had speared a couple of big fish, and we vented our wrath on them, in suitable fashion, for all the bites we'd endured in the water from the fish we didn't manage to catch. But there were no further snags that day, and toward evening we reached the Indian village where Francisco's cousin lived.

The first person to spot us was a woman, squatting down by the river to draw water. She ran scrambling up the slope, shouting the news in a loud voice. When we came ashore, the whole tribe had gathered to meet us. My presence at once sent the women scampering back to their huts, though they quickly began peeping out at me through chinks and crannies: their curiosity and their timid reticence were about equally balanced.

The community was made up of about fifty people. They were near-savages, dressed in the usual ragged clouts, generally of red material. They lived in large straw huts, which formed a circle around a central threshing floor. In the middle burned a fire that was never allowed to go out: it had a shed over it to protect it from bad weather.

They offered us smoked fish and pineapple to eat. Before we retired for the night Francisco came and told me that the following day we would reach the second cataract, a more difficult one than the first. It would be necessary to make a portage of canoe and gear by land. He had asked his cousin if he could lend us a couple of extra men to help with this portage. The men wanted five tins of sardines and a little salt.

"Very well," I told him. "If you think it's necessary."

"Yes, señor. It's necessary."

"Good night, then, Francisco."

"Good night, señor."

When dawn broke they all came down to the river with us, women included: the latter appeared to have plucked up courage overnight. There was one girl, with a flat, slim, adolescent figure, whose high breasts and erect nipples reminded me that I had been leading a celibate life for rather too long.

The two local men had their own canoe, which was made of bark and was an altogether faster and more rakish craft than ours. Very soon it was so far ahead that we lost sight of it. Shortly before noon we found its occupants sprawled out on the bank. Angelito lit a fire, and the two men produced a large palm leaf full of white grubs, each as big as a man's little finger. They impaled them on small sticks and set them to roast over the fire. Then they began to gobble them down avidly, till the fat literally dripped from their chins. The sight sickened me so much that I moved off and ate my own tin of meat at a little distance.

A little later we went into the forest in search of fruit. The Indian in front suddenly came to a halt. There, its bulging eyes fixed on us, was a giant spider: legs included, it must have measured nearly two feet across.

Francisco signaled to me that this was an occasion when my gun was called for.

"An *arañamono*," he told me, when I had duly shot the creature. "Very dangerous. Makes big jumps. Gives you a high fever and makes you die. It's a good thing you killed it, because it's a female."

I looked, and saw a pouch the size of a walnut hanging beneath the spider's belly, crammed with eggs. Francisco squashed the corpse with his bare foot.

The two other Indians meanwhile had been busily felling a small tree that was heavy with fruit, each growth the size of a man's fist. When they were halfway through the trunk, a

swarm of grubs like those they had eaten earlier came squirm-
ing out of the incision.

"Very good food," Francisco said, pointing at them. "White
men not like eating them at first. But when they try them, they
like them a lot."

Sure enough, when I brought myself to sample them, a few
months later, once I overcame my first instinctive repugnance
I found them excellent.

We reached the second lot of rapids with an hour and a
half of daylight still in hand. We beached the canoe and made
our way up the hillside, using the machetes to hack a path
through a fantastic tangled thicket of rank undergrowth and
twisting lianas. The Caroní dropped nearly a hundred feet at
this cataract, throwing up a fine cloud of spray all around:
even where we were we could feel it. As I glanced toward the
river I caught sight of a snake—it couldn't have been less than
twelve feet in length—coiled over a clutch of eggs: it faced us
threateningly, head and neck erect, thin darting tongue flick-
ering in and out of its open mouth.

Francisco came up at my call and put a restraining hand on
my arm.

"No point in shooting that," he said. "You don't want to
waste your bullets."

It was, I gathered, a large viper, with some very useful
habits, which included keeping down the mice, iguanas, and
crickets that tended to infest the huts. Snakes like this one
could be more or less tamed, and were kept in the villages,
often actually inside someone's home.

During our absence Angelito had caught a turtle. When we
got back the two new Indians were fetching flat stones and
laying them across the fire. Then the turtle was placed on the
stones. After several vain attempts to escape from its agonizing situation, the poor creature emerged from its shell, writhing and bleeding. One clean blow of a machete beheaded it.
The nausea caused by the day's culinary experiences was now
intensified by the horror that this cruel killing induced in me.
The physical manifestation of evil always turns my stomach.

But I was forced to admit that those turtle steaks were a real gourmet's dream.

During the night, for the first time, I heard the roar of a puma. One of the two Indians who lay stretched out by our campfire got up, threw some more wood on the flames, and went back to sleep again. The puma had come down to slake its thirst at the river; it continued to make the night air hideous with its angry roaring, but did not come anywhere near the camp.

Before ten o'clock on the fourth morning of our journey all our gear had been carried over the crest of the hill and down to the river again. We gave the two Indians a large breakfast and sent them back to their village. Then we launched the canoe once more. The broad and majestic river had shrunk to a narrow, fast-moving stream—so fast-moving, indeed, that at times, for all our paddling, we made no headway. When this happened one of the Indians would go overboard and push. On our left rose the mountains, home of apes and baboons; on our right, the jungle.

The place where we made camp that evening turned out to be infested with huge black ants, over two inches long, which came scuttling out as soon as we beached the canoe. They were the sort known by the Venezuelans as *ventiquatros,* since it is popularly believed that if they bite you, the limb in question is paralyzed for the next twenty-four hours. We moved on nearly a mile in order to get clear of them.

But our new site had its disadvantages, too. In the middle of the night I was wakened by the most fantastic uproar: it sounded as though some vast compact yet intangible multitude was on the point of converging on us. Francisco appeared to be asleep. But when I could stand it no longer, and sprang up, gun at the ready, he calmly remarked: "Nothing to be scared of, señor. Just *araguatos.*" He explained that these were a certain species of ape, about three feet tall, which went hunting food in packs. Except when eating or sleeping, they kept up this racket the whole time, it seemed; it was the only activity they knew. I have since heard that they are very tasty roasted.

At all events, they stopped my getting any more sleep that night, even after their noisy uproar had faded away in the distance.

A little later, in the middle of preparing coffee, José and Antonio suddenly snatched up their bows and charged off through the undergrowth, drawn by the faint call of a woodcock. Shortly afterward I heard the bird creating a furious diversion, in the vain hope of defending its young against attack. Finally, still squawking shrilly, it took to the air. An arrow pierced it clean through in mid-flight. It struggled on for a moment or so, but the wound and the weight of the arrow proved too much for it. Its wing-beats grew progressively feebler, and finally it plummeted down into the lagoon. With a few quick strokes Angelito swam out and retrieved it. When he got back to us the little bird was still palpitating.

Antonio and José between them brought the bag up to nine; but when we gathered for breakfast at the usual time, I refused to sample grilled woodcock. I have no doubt, however, that they were delicious.

Throughout the next night a chorus of bullfrogs croaked unceasingly, and the air was uneasy with the hunting cries of leopard and jaguar. The day that followed—our last on the Caroní—started badly and got worse as it went on.

The banks of the river rose to a sheer sixty feet in the gorge, jutting out slightly overhead. The rapids, some eight hundred yards long, fell in three successive cataracts. We stood on a spit below the gorge trying to think of a way to surmount this obstacle. Suddenly I heard a shout of pain. Angelito emerged from the water, one knee spurting blood. He had been perched on a rock, fishing; a big fish had taken his bait and dragged him into the river, where he had smashed his knee against a sharp underwater reef. I disinfected and bandaged the cut, but it was plain that he could not walk.

It was this that finally decided us in favor of attempting to steer the canoe up through the rapids rather than make a portage. We assumed the same positions as we had done the first time. Antonio and José hauled at the prow; Francisco kept the craft from swinging into the rocks on the right, while I, from the stern, did the same on the left. Angelito watched the operation but was unable to assist us in any way.

Despite all our efforts, the canoe swung dangerously off-course several times, and more than once we had to bail out the water it had shipped. After two hours, however, we had only ten yards or so to go, and I was just preparing to thank the Lord for seeing us through when the two Indians in front stopped and called out to Francisco.

We had not seen the last of our troubles yet. Ahead of us lay a pool, five yards and more across, too deep to get a foothold on the bottom and so haul the canoe through. The banks were too high and the ropes too short for us to think of clambering ashore and circumventing the obstacle that way. It looked as though there was only one solution. Somebody would have to swim across to the far side of the pool, and we would then throw the rope over to him.

Antonio plunged into the water. As soon as he reached the bank José tossed the rope at him, but it slipped out of his hand. The current was very strong, and the canoe began to swing around broadside on. Francisco shoved at it with all his might, but finally eased off for fear of its overturning. I at once belayed the stern rope around a projecting rock. With nothing to hold its bow steady, the canoe heeled over and capsized. Its contents spilled out into the water and were whirled away by the current.

When I recovered from my initial shock I spotted the waterproof bag bobbing about in the foam some thirty yards downstream. It contained my most vital equipment—compass, ammunition, medical supplies, matches, sugar, salt, and my clothes. I plunged off in pursuit and managed to catch up with it in the pool of slack water just above the third cataract.

When I staggered ashore and looked back, I perceived that I had been followed, at not more than a yard's distance, by several alligators. Bruised and out of breath, I toiled painfully back up the slope, the bag slung over my shoulder. Meanwhile the Indians had righted the canoe and rescued hammocks, blankets, bows, and arrows from the water.

It was easy enough to tow our *curiara* without its load; but we found it had sprung numerous leaks. While one of the Indians went off in search of cotton plants for material to plug these leaks, the rest of us returned to the scene of the catastrophe. I tied a rope around my waist and told one of my companions to keep hold of the loose end. The water was opaque and muddy from tannic deposits; I would have to fumble about on the bottom, below the surface, if I was going to recover any of those commonplace articles which to us, in our situation, had become so infinitely precious. At my fourth attempt I brought up a diamond sieve, but after that I retired winded. Francisco took over, and rescued a further two sieves. We went on like this, turn and turn about, till evening.

When we took stock of our equipment, missing items included the fishhooks (invaluable also as material to barter with the natives): only two had survived, entangled in one of the ropes. Rice, flour, and casabe were a total write-off, along with the hammer, two of our machetes, and a cooking pot.

It was out of the question to think of spending weeks on end exploring remote and uninhabited districts without either rice, casabe, or yuca flour: we could not rely entirely on wild fruit and local fish. Cardona had told me that a certain Indian tribe lived at the confluence of the Icaparú and Caroní Rivers: Francisco knew about this tribe, too. We would have to barter our salt with them in return for essential supplies.

With much laborious effort we hacked a path through the jungle, and by the evening of the following day we had got the canoe and all our surviving gear up past the rapids. The day after, our energy kept up by a diet of Angelito's fish, we paddled the mile or so that still lay between us and the Icaparú, turned off into its mouth, and beached our canoe on the left bank.

Chapter 4

◆

THE TAUREPÁN TRIBE

The tribe we were looking for must be somewhere in this area. It was impossible to go on without a supply of casabe, so we had to make contact with one of these Indians somehow. On the right-hand side of the river we could just descry the roofs of a group of huts, but there was no sign of life about them. In order to advertise our presence I finally decided to take a pot shot at one of a pair of *guachamay* flying overhead. These are giant parrots, with extremely vivid and multicolored plumage —red, blue, green, and yellow. They also make excellent eating. Hitherto I had not had the heart to kill one.

I aimed and fired: a clean hit. The survivor began to screech in so heart-rending a fashion that, by a process of human logic as cruel as it was disconcerting, I felt constrained to add him to the bag, too. Pity sometimes adopts such arguments, though they will not stand close inspection. The truth of the matter is that there are times when we cannot bear to be merciful.

My marksmanship had, however, accomplished its secondary purpose. Scarcely had the echoes of the two shots died way when five canoes moved out from the far bank; there were two men in each of them, all armed with bows and arrows. The appearance they presented was far from reassuring. Despite Francisco's repeated assertion that these were "good Indians," I loaded my gun and remained at a discreet distance from the point at which they would land.

They were of medium height, but very strongly built; their

near-nakedness was matched by an intense natural curiosity. They knew not a word of Spanish, but at once got on friendly terms with Francisco. Nevertheless all his questions were met by a stubborn shake of the head from their leader, though I saw him eying my hunting knife and rifle with open greed. Brushing Francisco's demands aside, he strode across to where I stood, obviously bent on taking my rifle off me. At first I resisted; then, reassured by Francisco's expression, I let him have it. He turned it over and examined it meticulously, with that characteristic stance and absorbed concentration which men handling guns display the world over. Then he made as though to aim at something with it, and handed it back again.

The discussion between Francisco and the locals now re-commenced. "They want to know the exact spot at which the canoe capsized," Francisco told me.

"Tell them I will point it out to them. Say that in exchange for three weeks' supply of casabe we will give them five boxes of matches, and three double handfuls of salt from our sack."

"He say they have very little casabe, and the yuca crop is still unripe."

This startled me. "What? Can't you make casabe with unripe yuca?"

"Oh yes, señor; but it uses up a lot of plants, and the harvest has been poor."

"Tell him they can have four double handfuls of salt."

But the old devil continued to shake his head in that obstinate way he had, all the time casting covert glances at my hunting knife. In the hope of bringing this long-drawn-out argument to a close, I finally drew it from my belt and held it out to Francisco. The chief summed up the situation in a flash; he grabbed the knife, tested its blade on his thumb, and muttered something.

"He says you can have the yuca," Francisco translated.

We were ferried across the river in the tribesmen's canoes, extremely light craft that always seemed on the point of over-turning. When we entered the village the women, who had been working on the threshing floor, vanished and hid themselves in the usual manner.

I hadn't had a woman since leaving Ciudad Bolívar, and this recurrent flight of all the local talent was beginning to make me feel unpleasantly frustrated. So much so, in fact, that when I saw one nice bare-breasted young girl ducking into what was clearly the chief's own hut I tagged along behind her, paying no attention to Francisco's efforts to restrain me.

The girl was kneeling on the floor beside a decrepit old crone who appeared to be on the point of death. I pretended an active concern for the dying woman, but continued to watch the girl out of the corner of my eye. She had shrunk away into a corner of the hut, terrified. The floor was strewn with dry bones (including fishbones) and scraps of casabe. Large numbers of ants swarmed over it in all directions. There was an appalling stench of filth and decomposing meat.

Francisco came and dragged me out, saying that the chief had provided a basket to put the yuca in. I asked him if the old woman on her deathbed was the chief's wife.

"Yes, señor: his wife."

"And the girl?"

"She's his wife, too, señor."

The thought of this gorgeous dark-skinned girl being the property of a dirty old patriarch like the chief was utterly repulsive to me; and my prolonged sexual abstinence merely served to increase my feelings of disgust. But it was not the appropriate moment for broaching this sort of problem. The most important thing just now was the yuca. The field was some way off, and we set off toward it at a brisk pace.

The yuca is a poisonous tuber that can grow to the size of an eggplant, sometimes even bigger. The fact of its being poisonous is extremely fortunate for the forest tribesmen, since animals cannot eat it, whereas they have discovered a means of turning it into a staple item of their diet simply by pounding the roots and squeezing out the toxic juices.

We filled a basket with yuca roots, but the old chief, who was in a testy and distrustful mood, would not allow us to pound them up and prepare our casabe on the spot; so that evening, back in camp, we had perforce to contrive makeshift graters of our own from the tins we opened for supper. With such implements, it was clear, we could not produce overmuch casabe from the modest store of yuca at our disposal; and in any case we would have to stay put for a couple of days till it dried out. So that this period should not be altogether wasted, we decided to spend our time hunting and fishing; thus with luck we would have a fair supply of provisions when we set off again.

We began that same night. According to Francisco, conditions were favorable: it had not rained for some time, the forest pools were dried up, and the animals were obliged to come down to the river to drink. Our best plan was to paddle a few miles up the Icaparú, and then return, letting the current carry us downstream. The river was fairly narrow, and we stood a good chance of sighting some game on the banks that was within range of our canoe.

"I can always spot them," Francisco told me. "I see their eyes glinting. When I touch your shoulder, you shoot."

Huge screech owls swooped low overhead, in search of their own prey. All along the riverbanks the alligators lay in wait, ready to pounce on the jungle animals when they came down to drink. Vast swarms of vampire bats fluttered around us like so many black ghosts.

Francisco was in the bow, Antonio at the stern, and I amidships. When the Southern Cross came up over the horizon we pushed off into midstream, shipped our paddles, and let the canoe drift with the current. I sat close beside Francisco now, my rifle cocked and ready. I saw the occasional glint of an eye in the undergrowth, but Francisco made no sign. Then, at last, a pair of yellow sparks gleamed out at us, I felt a quick tap on my shoulder, took aim, and fired. Francisco was over the side and had retrieved my victim almost before the echoes of the shot had died away. He dumped it in the bottom of the canoe: it turned out to be a young *lapa*. This is an animal that comes out only at night; its flesh is tasty and plentiful—a good specimen can weigh anything up to seventeen or eighteen pounds. On three further occasions Francisco touched my shoulder; once I missed, but with the other two shots I killed a roebuck and an *acurí*, the latter being a member of the rodent family about the size of a hare.

By noon the following day we had succeeded in making about two dozen rounds of casabe. At this point the local tribal chief arrived by canoe. He brandished my knife and insisted on Angelito's going with him to point out the spot where our own canoe had capsized. Nothing else would satisfy him, try as we might.

At dawn on the eleventh day after our departure from Uriman we finally resumed our journey, moving southward still, upriver, ever deeper into the heart of the jungle. The Icaparú rises on the borders of Brazil and British Guiana, and flows northwest across the Gran Sabana. It is about sixty feet wide, and between rapids flows so calmly that it resembles a canal. We were making for a small tributary of the Icaparú, the Hacha, known by the Indians as the Paracupí, and reckoned on reaching it in four days at the outside; as things turned out, we took a week. While we were navigating one of the numerous rapids, the canoe capsized again, and developed several leaks as a result: we had to stop every hour to bail it out. Our stock of fish and meat went bad, and the casabe was practically exhausted. On the fourth day we lost our one remaining big fishhook. All we had left was a tiny affair which we cast for hours on end to produce one small panful of fish.

My men were now in an extremely sour mood. They followed me, against their will, simply because I had managed to win their loyalty; they paddled on like galley slaves in an effort to get me as near my destination as possible; but Francisco had already hinted that it was high time to turn back. On the other hand the thick green leafy vault of foliage overhead made paddling less irksome a task, forming a welcome protection against the direct rays of the sun. Here and there we saw a completely bare tree—an odd, wintry phenomenon, out of place in a landscape where every square inch of soil seemed to nurture some living growth. These trees indicated the presence of *pereza* monkeys in the vicinity: the species is very plentiful in these parts. The word *pereza* means idleness, and the monkeys get their name from a habit they have of descending on one tree and staying there till they have stripped every leaf and green shoot off it.

We reached the mouth of the Hacha at dusk on the seventh day, and it was then that Francisco spoke seriously of their turning back. Even I accepted the fact that they could not accompany me farther; indeed, I was hard put to it on occasion to master my own fear and anxiety. But one thing kept me going: I felt I had come too far to give up at this stage.

According to Cardona's information, when I had reached the Hacha I was to paddle up it for two days or so, at which time I should observe a still smaller tributary on the western side. From here I was to continue southward by foot. After a day's march I should have reached the foothills of a big mountain range, on the far side of which was the Rio Blanco and the beginning of Taurepán territory.

"You can't leave me yet," I told Francisco. "Not with so far to go still."

The poor Indian desperately wanted to go back home, but it seemed a breach of loyalty to leave me alone in such a dangerous situation.

"We'll stay here tomorrow," I said, feeling him waver and doing my best to make up his mind in my favor. "We'll repair the canoe and lay in a supply of fresh food. After that you can keep on with me just for another two days. All right?"

Francisco made no immediate reply, but retired to confer with his friends. Finally he came and told me that they agreed to carry on for another two days, but without any initial delay. (When things are inevitable, one just shrugs and accepts them; there's no alternative.) But, he reminded me, we were almost out of casabe, our tinned food was running very low too, and for several days now we had not had enough to eat. It was absolutely essential to lay our hands on food of some sort.

Sundown is not exactly the best time to go hunting. By then those animals that are up and about during the day have already retired, and their nocturnal brethren are not yet on the prowl. Nevertheless we set off into the jungle, urged on by the need to find some tufts of cotton to calk the canoe—if nothing else. But we were lucky enough also to run across a young ant bear, which assuaged our mounting pangs of hunger.

As our hunger diminished, so did our ill-humor. The following day, after we had roasted all the tastier joints of the bear, we set off up the Hacha. It was a miserable little stream, full of dead leaves and silted up with mud; it barely avoided being swallowed up altogether by the encroaching jungle. Frequently we had to get out the machetes and hack our way through. As we advanced the stream gradually shrank, and at several points the water became so shallow that we were forced to disembark to keep the canoe afloat. To make things even more difficult, there were numerous rapids. I began to fear that two days was an overoptimistic estimate for the time it would take us to reach the little stream on Cardona's map. With this in mind I continually urged the Indians to paddle faster, and helped them as best I could myself.

The high degree of humidity made the air dense and hard to breathe. Myriad swarms of gnats, mosquitoes, and flies of every description danced hypnotically before our eyes and stung us all over, so that we writhed in perpetual agony. One insect, indeed, found its way into my right ear, and the more desperately I tried to shake it out again, the deeper it penetrated. A noise rather like a whole squadron of aircraft landing buzzed through my brain, and my head seemed to explode. The only reason I came around again, I felt, was to discover whether I was about to die or just going crazy. Finally Francisco grasped what was going on, though I was no longer capable of speaking, and acted at once. He rolled up a leaf into a funnellike shape, and made me pass water into it. Then he bent my head sideways and poured the urine into the ear concerned. The buzzing lessened instantly, and a moment later all was quiet. I felt restored to life again. If this, I told myself, was the Green Hell, what I had just been through was one of its tortures for the damned.

It was dusk on the third day before we reached the stream. We divided the provisions that still remained between us. My share was two rounds of casabe, four tins of meat, two of sardines, two of lard, and a mere handful of coffee. The Indians adamantly refused to leave me the one remaining fishhook. At the very last moment, when they had their paddles raised to move off, Francisco jumped out of the canoe, pulled his hunting knife from his belt, and gave it to me.

"You'll need it, señor," he said.

I stood watching them for as long as I could follow their progress through the tangling foliage, and kept my ears strained to catch the fading *scloop* of their paddles in the water. When the last faint ripple whispered and was gone, I could feel the jungle, with all its mysteries, encircling and pressing in on me. I remembered tales I had heard from the *purgüeros,* the workers who collect latex deposits in the rubber forests: tales of the jungle-sickness, a kind of *cafard* which never leaves a man once it has struck him, the dizzy horror of mile upon mile of uniform rubber trees, imprisoning these human intruders in an infinite silent universe, a cage of receding trunks, till the brain rebels and explodes with lunatic ferocity, against one's companions, against oneself. During all the time I had spent traveling my mind had been exclusively occupied with countless immediate practical problems, and focused, beyond them, on the ultimate goal ahead of me. Though Francisco and his men knew the route, and the navigational hazards, much better than I did—I was entering, after all, an unknown world—nevertheless I felt that the final responsibility for the entire expedition was mine.

But now, once again, I realized how much the presence of fellow creatures may mean. I was physically too exhausted to experience the elation that normally goes with risky undertakings tackled alone, a spur that had driven me so often in the past, and launched me on so many unpremeditated departures. The first time it happened to me I was still more or less a child. After one rather more than usually extended escapade (on which I had had a friend with me) my father decided to pack me off to a seminary. I don't know whether he thought he had detected signs of a religious vocation in me, or simply felt that the discipline would do me good. I lived like a prisoner in a vast, gloomy building of considerable antiquity, and looked forward to the periods set aside for meditation or private study, when I could closet myself in my own small room, which was rather like a monk's cell. The desk was beneath the window. I would spread out a big atlas on it and mark lines in red pencil from San Francisco to Tokyo, Miami to Sydney, Dakar to Rome, or Moscow, or Shanghai, losing myself in endless traveler's daydreams. Yet this did not stop me, during services or in the classroom, from also experiencing intermittent bursts of genuine religious ardor.

From my cell window I could see a tree, and on this tree one particular sparrow regularly perched. Occasionally I would interrupt my private fantasies to scatter crumbs on the window sill, and watch the sparrow hop over and peck them up. One day the sparrow arrived with a companion. They set about the crumbs for a while, then began to chase each other. It looked as though they were quarreling, and I watched in fascination, trying not to lose sight of them even when they fluttered off back to the tree. Then, suddenly, something clicked in my mind, sharp as the fall of a portcullis: I seemed to sense an elusive air of complicity between these two sparrows, and in a flash I knew, with sudden, unlooked-for awareness, that they were not quarreling, and that my own true vocation did not lie in the direction of priestly chastity. I went down into the garden (luckily, it was siesta-time and no one was stirring), clambered over the wall, and began to run across country, as fast as I could. Finally I struck a railway line, and followed it to the nearest station, where I hitched a ride on a troop train.

The infinite silence weighed on my heart like a gravestone. I tried to steel myself against the onset of fear; yet at the same time endless rational arguments why I should not resume my journey immediately, or indeed move out of earshot of the water, came crowding into my mind. Finally convinced by logic inspired by fear, I decided to spend that night where I was. To keep my guilt feeling at bay, I got everything ready for a dawn departure the following morning. I rolled myself up in my net before darkness actually fell, in order to keep those tormenting swarms of mosquitoes at bay. The great screech owls circled around me, and from time to time one of them would swoop down for a closer look. If I had been a *lapa* or even a roebuck, this would undoubtedly have proved my last night on earth.

At first light I got up, stuffed all my possessions into the waterproof bag, strapped the sieves and crowbar on top of it, and slung it from my back like a rucksack. Then, with my rifle in my left hand, a machete in my right, and the compass hung around my neck, I set forth on a solitary march that was to last four days.

Every square inch of my body was swollen from countless insect bites. I had always to be on my guard, too, against that other deadly peril of the South American jungle, poisonous snakes, or *quaima,* as the natives call them. A couple of seconds' absent-mindedness may mean treading on one, with fatal consequences. During the first day I avoided several snakes in the nick of time, giving them a wide berth so as not to rouse them. But one I spotted too late, and actually grazed with my foot. It squirmed away from me, reared its head, and began to follow in my tracks. I hoped it would change direction after a moment or two; but it came straight on, so I knocked it on the head with the butt of my rifle.

With the return of daylight my terrors of the previous evening vanished. Once again I was so keyed up for my immediate task—the anticipation and circumvention of all dangerous hazards—that my fertile imagination could no longer find a breeding ground. I pushed on briskly—as briskly, that is, as the terrain would allow. On the second day, however, something happened which scared me half out of my wits. I had already reached the lower slope of the range beyond which lay my goal, the Rio Blanco. I was just casting around for a suitable spot to light my evening fire when the silence was shattered by an ear-splitting, weirdly human cry, that echoed back from the mountains ahead of me. For a moment I froze in my tracks. My first thought was that this must be the war cry of some savage jungle tribe. I hesitated, then, with a conscious effort, forced myself to turn back in the direction from which the sound had come. Ten yards or so down the track I perceived the real source of it. There lay a wretched ape, pinned flat and struggling under the weight of the jaguar that had pounced on it from some overhanging branch. Instinctively, to bolster my courage rather than from necessity, I emptied five rounds—my entire magazine—into them, killing both straight off. Then it occurred to me that I myself, a moment or so before, had passed beneath the tree in which the jaguar crouched waiting; at the thought cold sweat broke out on my face and my back, while my entire body began to tremble convulsively. The one thing that kept me going (a frail enough support, at that) was the hope that I had almost completed my journey. But when I reached the summit of the pass next day, there before me lay a seemingly endless *meseta,* or mountain plateau, stretching away to the far horizon.

This time my despair was complete and absolute; there was no way out of this impasse. I could not turn back alone. I had no idea how much farther I would have to struggle on before I met another human being. My casabe was finished; I had two tins of meat left, and one of sardines. There was no sign of water anywhere: the first pangs of thirst had already begun to attack me. Physical weakness made me a prey to torturing hallucinations, and the onset of darkness merely served to increase my misery. If it had been even remotely possible to press on through the forest at night, I should have done so; as it was, I got moving again at the first hint of dawn. I hacked away at the undergrowth before me with the desperate energy of one who no longer has anything to lose. The vegetation was not so thick as it had been, and I was not obliged to use my machete the whole time.

After several hours of this I came across some fresh game spoors, which meant that there was bound to be water not too far off. About midday I halted to cook one of the two rabbits I had bagged en route. While I was eating it I thought I could hear a faint, far-off murmuring sound. Heart pounding madly, I strained my ears for a moment, then sprang up and ran on for three or four hundred yards. The sound was clearer now, rather like the hum you get when you hold a shell to your ear.

Water, it must be water, it couldn't be anything else—a stream, a river, fresh, flowing, beautiful water!

I went back, finished the rabbit, and collected my gear. Another three hours' walking brought me to the edge of the plateau, and I had my first glimpse down into the valley below. Like some great coiling serpent the Rio Blanco lay there, glittering in the sunlight, issuing from a deep gorge between two mountain peaks.

I raised my arms heavenward and went bounding down the slope. Hunger, thirst, exhaustion, mosquito bites—all were forgotten. Beyond that river were human beings, savages perhaps, but living people, men like myself. I began to rehearse the little speech I would make—in their dialect—at our first encounter. It seemed just right, and I felt I had mastered words and accent well enough. But I also had to consider a second possibility, that of running into members of some other, less friendly tribe, when I might well forget the whole thing through panic, and get an arrow through me before I could open my mouth. At this point, perhaps providentially, I stumbled, and had my mind jerked out of its gloomy forebodings. During the past few days I had become a past master at such extravagantly pessimistic conjectures.

Dusk was falling by the time I reached the riverbank, and I was completely out of breath. I threw down all my gear and plunged into the water, joyful as only a man can be who has survived many hazards and won through at long last to freedom. It was so wonderful to be able to drink again, to refresh one's whole body with water, that I quite forgot all the unknown perils that still lay ahead of me.

Next morning I observed a tall tree that leaned out over the surface of the water, and was long enough—supposing I felled it—to reach the farther bank and form a sort of footbridge. I could never have waded across with all my gear.

The wood turned out to be extremely hard. It cost me several hours' labor, considerable muscle-strain, and two intervals for sharpening up my blunted machete, before the tree finally dropped, with a mighty crash, onto the far bank, sending up clouds of flies and gnats as it settled. The perils I had come through all forgotten, I once more kindled into excitement at the thought of being so near my goal. I decided to rest for a little while, wash out my clothes, and have a shave. The river was full of fish, which came darting up under the bank where I stood, as though deliberately tantalizing me. Since I had no fishhooks, I toyed for a moment with the idea of using my mosquito net as a sort of trawl; but I soon dismissed this notion. The protection the mosquito net afforded me was far too precious to risk losing it. I made do with the remaining rabbit.

The next morning I got my equipment safely across. It took me three separate trips. I was just about to set foot on the far side for the third time when four naked and devilish-looking figures emerged in front of me, bows bent, long arrows aimed in my direction. I knew that their tips were steeped in a poison capable of paralyzing the entire nervous system through one minute puncture. But in the last resort these creatures were fellow human beings; at that moment I felt disposed to treat even apparently hostile savages as my brothers. They were, in fact, the first Taurepán tribesmen I met.

I stood where I was and managed to articulate the sentence I had been practicing, and which had triggered off such conflicting expectations in my mind.

"Me friend of big chief Mundo," I said.

By way of response one of the savages relieved me of my rifle, cartridge belt, and hunting knife. The others humped all my equipment onto their shoulders—that was one advantage, anyhow—and we set off in Indian file, two of them in front, two behind, with me in the middle, along a track that ran beside the river.

Their only garment was an exiguous loincloth. They had curly, jet-black hair, somewhat almond-shaped eyes, and very dark skin. All four of them were built like athletes. There was nothing about their bearing or conduct that gave the least clue as to their possible intentions. I felt that it could, in any case, do no harm to break the silence, so I brought out Mundo's photograph and showed it to the two behind me. They muttered something to each other which I failed to catch. So I laboriously repeated my introductory greeting in their tongue. "Me friend of Mundo," I said. "Me see Mundo."

They took the photograph from me, too. Clearly these were people who preferred dealing in hard facts.

About an hour later we stopped by a little stream. One of them brought out some casabe from the pouch attached to his girdle: I was given my share like the rest. It must have been midafternoon when we emerged on a ridge from where we could see the Rio Blanco below us again, at its point of juncture with another river, the Uai-parú. Beyond it clustered the roofs of the Taurepáns' huts.

Chapter 5

•

MUNDO

Coming into this Taurepán village was rather like being transported back to the Stone Age. Their artifacts were incredibly primitive: wooden spears, stone vessels, clumsily woven straw baskets, flint axes. The huts stood on the right-hand side of the river, around a wide central square. Some of them were bigger than the rest, and seemed to have been built with greater care. My escort vanished into one of these more substantial dwellings, taking almost all my baggage with them, and leaving me outside on the threshold.

Hardly were they out of sight, however, when I was surrounded by a crowd of naked children, together with one or two women whose sole article of attire was a loincloth secured by a length of liana knotted around the waist. They stared at me in fascination, poking and prodding me all over, accompanying their inspection with remarks to me and to one another that I could not understand, and pointing out various special physical features, my beard in particular.

So eager were the women to examine and touch me that they had abandoned their cooking fire out in the middle of the square, where they had been roasting a brace of iguanas alive. One of these wretched creatures—though burned nearly to a crisp—had rolled off into the embers after a series of agonized contortions, and was now painfully attempting to drag itself clear of the fire altogether. I pointed this out to the women.

They thought it a fine joke, and began to laugh heartily. Then several of them ran over to the iguana, and carefully replaced it on its grid of torment. I spent a moment or two trying to stifle the suspicion that I was quite liable to finish up the same way.

I was finally rescued from the inquisitive fingers of all these women and children by the reappearance of the four warriors. They were preceded by a dignified and impressive old man, who bore himself as straight as a ramrod; the rags he wore draped around his shoulders were just recognizable as the remains of an old shirt. Behind him there came a most enchanting young girl, who, as was the custom with all the women in this tribe, had her breasts exposed.

Inactive and without means of communication as I had been during the past hours, my mind had become somewhat numbed, liable only to be alerted by the threat of danger, against which I remained constantly on my guard, ignorant though I might be of its precise nature. But the sight of this girl gave a most agreeable jolt to my responses. I am not suggesting that so vague a stimulus did much, *per se*, to lift me out of the brutish state of insensitivity into which I seemed to have sunk; but at all events I realized that this was something more than a purely physical reaction brought about by my unsatisfied sexual appetites. Over and above the girl's bodily attractions—which certainly were responsible for the element of sheer pleasure in my reaction to her—I seemed once more to discern the possibility of communicating with a fellow creature, of establishing a mode of intercourse that hitherto my ignorance of the local dialect had precluded.

At sight of the old man everyone withdrew. Holding Mundo's photograph in his hand, and addressing himself to me, he mumbled a few unintelligible words, to which I could only reply with my usual litany: "Me see Mundo. Me friend Mundo. Me talk Mundo."

He indicated that I was to go inside the hut with him. Here I found the entire contents of my bag strewn over the floor. Patiently I set about picking everything up and stowing it away again, except for a shirt, which I offered to the old man.

He looked at me in some surprise, I thought, but nevertheless lost no time in putting it on over the rags he wore already.

Throwing out his chest and quite clearly in an excellent mood, the old fellow now harangued his four warriors. Three of them at once took off into the forest, presumably to look for the rest of their companions, who were, it seemed, out hunting with Mundo. Meanwhile the news of my arrival had spread abroad, and when I emerged from the hut I found various new groups of women waiting for me, all surrounded by their offspring, all there for the express purpose of scrutinizing and prodding my person. For the first time on this trip I was up against women who, far from running away and hiding, were talking to me without embarrassment and even with a hint of excitement.

The village was built to a remarkably symmetrical plan. Each hut had its own threshing floor and a path leading down to the river. Their framework consisted of bamboo poles, anything from three to six inches in diameter. The walls were made from strips of rough wood held together with woven lianas, and the steeply sloping roofs consisted of overlapping palm leaves: there is a certain dwarf palm which grows very plentifully in the surrounding forest. Though the smell of the whole place was extremely unpleasant, nevertheless its inhabitants—as I subsequently observed—were in the habit of bathing several times a day. They took scrupulous care of their persons, and were very clean and neat.

The warrior in charge of me, Taivan, marched close on my heels, armed with a blowpipe. I asked him the name of every object that came under my eye and tried my best to commit his answers to memory. The first step in gaining the confidence of these people was, clearly, to learn their language as quickly as possible.

When we reached the river we still had a long string of women trailing along behind us: they proceeded to plunge into the water with cheerful abandon. Suddenly I caught sight of the girl, standing there dripping wet with the old man. She was tall and dark-skinned: her eyes met mine, and she gazed steadily at me, with a strange expression of warmth and ten-

derness. Though she could not have been more than twelve
years old, she was, self-evidently, a woman.

With an effort I mastered the longing and the desire that
came surging violently up in me, and forced myself to concentrate on the real object of my journey. This river flowing
past at my feet was the river of diamonds I had come to find—
though a far cry from the fantastic stream that I had gradually
built up in my imagination. For a moment I was stricken with
fear: I felt the whole thing was an illusion, a mirage. Impatience mounted in me till, stupidly determined to reassure
myself, I plunged down to the bottom and scooped up two
fistfuls of mud, convinced that they would contain an unan-
swerable refutation of my fears. Naturally, nothing of the sort
happened: diamonds lie embedded deep in the gravel under a
river bed, not loose on the bottom.

On our way back to the village Taivan stooped down from
time to time and picked up an insect very much like the
scarabaeus, or dung beetle. He pulled off its legs and proceeded to eat them with every sign of relish, throwing away
the still living beast. Every so often he would offer one to me,
and derive childish enjoyment from my refusal. Between one
beetle and the next I did manage to extract some information
from him, however. The old man to whom I had presented a
shirt was the tribal shaman, the Sapulí as they called him, a
mixture of priest, medicine man, and magician. The girl's name
was Lolomai; she was not his wife, but his daughter. I cheered
up at this, as invariably happens when one's unformulated
hopes receive what seems to be a sign of encouragement.

On the village square several women were tending a large
stone bowl in which some whitish liquid was boiling. A little
way beyond them sat a mother suckling her baby on one
breast, and keeping the other for a small *chigüire.* The *chigüire* is an animal with extremely tasty flesh; the natives catch
it before it is weaned, and fatten it up in this pleasantly domestic fashion till it attains the right degree of plumpness and
tenderness.

That night I fell asleep to visions of the delectable and
disturbing Lolomai. Next morning, as soon as the sun was up,

women and children set off in all directions into the forest, carrying baskets, to search for fruit, roots, snails, edible snakes, berries, wild honey, turtles' eggs, and birds' nests.

Early in the afternoon a great barking of dogs heralded Mundo's return. He had a score or so of men behind him, carrying roebucks, *lapas,* and *báquiros,* the latter being a species of South American wild pig, large herds of which roam the territory adjacent to the Guianas. They weigh anything up to a hundred and fifty pounds. The smaller variety of this pig, or peccary, is sometimes known by the natives as *cháchari.* When they reached the village square the men dumped their burdens on the ground: from this point on the game became a distaff responsibility.

While the women were taking over the game, however, two of the hunters, indifferent to all but their immediate needs, hastily grabbed their wives, dragged them off by the hair, and proceeded to copulate with them in broad daylight, while the entire village looked on. Clearly the primitive and idyllic life of the Taurepán tribe still had a few surprises in store for me; and as things turned out, this was neither the last nor the biggest of them.

Mundo was a tall man, with heavy features that could express an extraordinarily wide range of moods, from stony ferocity to a certain melancholy gentleness. He seemed to take my presence very much for granted. After a leisurely dip in the river he strolled across toward me, his men trailing after him, all talking at once.

"You friend of Cardona?" Mundo finally asked me, in Spanish.

I told him yes, and reminded him that Cardona was his friend, too.

"He send you here?"

"Yes, he send me to see you. He tell me give you his greeting."

"Why you come this place?"

I brought out and showed him the second photograph, the one in which he was standing beside Cardona, together with a page from an illustrated magazine in which the same picture was reproduced.

"What this say?" Mundo asked, jabbing his finger at the text.

"It says you are big wise chief, friend of white man. White man know he can rely on you. Great White Chief who is lord of all men has seen this picture. One day he will come to find you."

While the rest of them huddled together, rolling their eyes and jabbering away in throaty gutturals, Mundo himself remained lost in thought, withdrawn and remote. But when he mechanically flipped over the page, revealing a picture of two glamorous white women, all hell broke loose. Countless hands reached out to grab the paper and get a first look at it. If it had not been for the energetic intervention of Mundo, roused from his absent spell, what began as fun might have degenerated into a serious fight.

But he barked a few orders, and the hubbub instantly subsided. Then he moved off briskly in the direction of the Sapulí's hut. The moment we were inside he laid hold of my rifle and cartridge belt, with the air of one who has an incontrovertible right to his own possessions. Then he beckoned to a boy and made him follow behind with the rest of my gear. We took one of the numerous paths till we reached a spacious enclosure, with one hut at each of its four corners and a fifth in the middle. This was Mundo's palace.

The boy put down my bag and slunk away.

"What you got in there?" Mundo asked.

I was surprised he had not got around to asking me this earlier.

"I would have brought you many presents," I said, "but the *curiara* I traveled in capsized twice in the big river. Lots of my stores and equipment were lost."

I showed him the little that remained: two boxes of ammunition, with fifty cartridges in each box; some medical supplies, one sieve, a shovel and crowbar, a canvas bucket, my *chinchorro* and blanket, a frying pan, three pairs of pants, five vests, and ten boxes of matches. I offered him a new pair of pants and a shirt. He put them on at once, and for the first time I saw him actually smile. The shirt is the gift of civilization most appreciated by the natives.

I had often tried to imagine what sort of person Mundo would turn out to be, but none of my conjectures came anywhere near the mark. He was a tough, suspicious, strong-willed character, and—which I found most unexpected of all—profoundly antagonistic toward all white men. This unwelcome discovery chilled my overhasty hopes of winning his sympathy from the start. To judge from his present attitude, there was every reason to fear that he might well send me on my way again, minus the rifle he had confiscated. Without either weapons or escort I had no hope of getting safely back the way I had come.

Mundo took good care to make me realize that my status was that of a prisoner—his prisoner. He buckled on my cartridge belt, stuck my knife through it, and with my rifle in his hand declared: "This gun mine."

If I was to avoid the complete ruination of my plans, I simply had to display a little firmness at this point myself.

"It will be yours," I retorted, "but only when I have completed my mission and am ready to return to my own great and powerful country."

"You leave when I say you leave. You thank your God you still alive. If you had been carrying gun when you met my warriors, you would be feeding fish of Rio Blanco now. I give order: kill all white men with guns."

This was the gist of the harangue that Mundo made to me in his broken Spanish, with a depth of sullen rancor the motive for which I very soon learned: it appeared that his only son, named Alabimu, had been killed by Europeans when on an expedition to carry off women from another tribe, ten days' march to the south. He and his companions had been surprised by a group of armed miners, who came to the assistance of the tribe they were raiding. Alabimu had failed to return.

"Listen, Mundo," I told him, "I have not come here to make trouble. I want to help your people. This territory of yours contains certain stones that are of very great interest to the white man. Perhaps the time is not far off when Europeans will come here in their hundreds, in their thousands even, and then you will be helpless to protect your people against these foreigners. They have enough guns to wipe you all out in the twinkling of an eye."

"I know, I know," Mundo said testily. "That is why I want no white men here. We want to live in peace, as our fathers did before us. I should kill you here and now."

"If you allow me to stay, no other white men will come here —and one day your people will have all that they could ever want. By helping me you will help your people. And the great chief Cardona will bring you many presents."

Cardona's name had more effect than all my threadbare rhetoric.

"When Cardona coming?"

"I do not know. But I do know he is interceding on your behalf with the Great White Chief. Maybe we will see him again very soon."

"You sleep here," was Mundo's only reply, and he marched out of the hut wearing my clothes and hung about with my weapons.

Fires had been lit out on the threshing floor in order to smoke the meat brought home by the hunters. This would give the tribe about three weeks' reserve. Lolomai was not among the women there. I went back to the hut and sat brooding over the situation. Presently Mundo reappeared, with some casabe and a portion of roasted meat. He stretched himself out on a mat without saying a word. Then, after contemplating the roof for a little while, he remarked: "My nephew Antu is ill. He was well when he came back from hunting with me. Now he will not eat, and he is cold even close to the fire."

Clearly he had a fever.

"Do you want me to look at him?"

"No. The Sapulí will not allow it."

"But the boy is your nephew. The medicine man cannot object, surely?"

"He is his son," Mundo said, "his son by my sister."

"Ah. Then he is Lolomai's brother?"

He looked sharply at me, frowning with suspicion.

"When have you seen Lolomai?"

"Yesterday. Taivan told me her name."

"I had a son," Mundo said, "a tall, strong, brave son. They killed him. They killed my son."

"I'm sorry, Mundo. I'm truly sorry about your son."

"I married twenty wives," he cried, raising clenched fists. "I wanted sons, many sons. But I have sired only daughters. I am ashamed."

"But that's not your fault," I said, foolishly. He gave no sign of having heard.

"When Lolomai was born," he went on, "we betrothed her to my son. But my son is dead and I shall not live much longer. So then Antu will be chief in my place. Antu is very wise and very brave. He has taken my son's place in my own heart, and with the whole tribe. Now he is sick, and I am afraid."

I slipped silently into my hammock. Mundo still lay there, staring up at the roof.

When I awoke the next morning the sun was already well up above the horizon. Where Mundo had been a big snake now lay coiled. It might possibly be one of those domesticated snakes that Francisco had told me about, but I could not be certain, and I hoped someone would appear and remove so irksome a hazard for me. But finally I got tired of lying there staring at the thing, so I slipped on my boots as fast as I could and hurried out. The snake never stirred.

Some of the women were still busy smoking meat on the central square. Others were pegging out the hides to dry in the sun. The whole village lay wrapped in primeval peace. I went down to the river to freshen up.

On my return I found the villagers all clustering around two Indians who had that moment arrived. Something serious must be in the wind, I thought: Mundo was in a thoroughly bad temper, and making no attempt to conceal the fact. With obvious irritation he snapped out several orders, and then stumped off to his hut. He aimed a vicious kick at the snake, which looped sluggishly out into the open.

"What's happened?" I asked him.

"Our people," he replied. "Two hours' march from here. Plant yuca."

"But what happened?"

"Kaicusé come last night, kill a woman."

Kaicusé is the name given by the Indians to any big cat.

"This the third time," Mundo said. "If Kaicusé once taste human flesh, he never stop. We must kill him."

As he spoke he had laid his hand on my rifle.

"It will be better if I come with you," I said. "The gun is dangerous. You do not understand how to work it. I will help you kill Kaicusé."

Ten minutes later we were on our way, straight past the village, together with eight other men. As we marched along the line of the river, Mundo told me the first victim had been a child who strayed out of its hut at night. When its parents had waited in vain for it to come back, they finally set out in a search party, carrying torches. They found the animal's tracks and some bloodstains. Next morning they organized a beat, but without result. A few days later a woman was slaughtered while she lay asleep with her whole family around her. These huts have no doors, and the Indians sleep packed together around a central hearth, in concentric circles: the children lie nearest the fire, the women next to them, and the men on the outside. The beast had leaped over the first circle and torn the poor woman's throat out before she even had time to cry for help. Then it had carried her away. In the morning none of the family had at first noticed the old woman's absence. It was only later that they found spatters of blood on the matting, and footprints similar to those seen the day the child disappeared. The beast in question was a male jaguar, fully grown and obviously of great daring.

Once again all attempts to hunt it down had failed, and people began to show signs of alarm. What they were dealing with, it was whispered, was Canaima in person, the Evil One himself. The medicine man had been summoned, and he proceeded to imprison the evil spirit in a tree trunk, which was then burned; its ashes were carefully collected and scattered in the river. For about three weeks everything was quiet, and the Indians became convinced that the magician's exorcism had got rid of Kaicusé. But the beast had returned yesterday, Mundo told me, and killed another old woman as she was coming home from the yuca-field, with a full basket on her head and two of her nieces accompanying her. The attack had been so swift and silent that the girls had no idea what had happened till they saw the basket rolling on the ground at their feet.

When we arrived, all eyes were turned hopefully on my rifle. Panic-stricken, the villagers showed us the remains of the third victim, which lay where the jaguar had left her, abandoning its prey when it heard men and dogs approaching. It was easy to see why this "beat"—and the other two—had not proved more successful.

"Mundo," I said, "if you send out men and dogs into the forest, Kaicusé will hear the noise they make and run far away. Then, when you have gone, he will come back and claim more victims. You must find another way of dealing with him. For instance, you can make him come here to you. If we carry the old woman's remains back to the spot where he left them, Kaicusé is bound to return to finish his meal—and then we will shoot him."

Mundo was instantly convinced by my argument. I knew from experience gained hunting elsewhere, in Siam and Cambodia, that the great cats have a very poorly developed sense of smell, though they are very keen-sighted and acute of hearing. All we had to do was conceal ourselves about ten yards away from the body, in such a position that we could not miss our target; our success would then depend simply on keeping quite still and quiet.

I had a trench dug at the edge of a thicket, and lined the bottom of it with cut grass. Then we waited till night fell, doing our best to reassure the women and children of the little community, who wanted to abandon their homes and return to the main body of the tribe.

When evening came we took up our position and lay waiting. I placed great reliance on Mundo's keen sense of hearing,

90144

and we had agreed that at the first rustle he was to put one hand on my shoulder. Despite the gathering darkness the old woman's remains were still clearly visible.

After a while I began to feel slightly less tense and expectant, and my mind strayed back over the events of the past few days, picking up fragmentary memories, though I was not really calm enough to recall any one of them in its entirety. Then, suddenly, Mundo tapped me on the shoulder. I strained my ears, but could hear nothing. Mundo's hand pressed harder. I turned my head. He indicated with a gesture that the beast was behind us. I kept quite still. After a second or two Mundo bent forward and whispered: "He's here."

Next morning we found his tracks. The jaguar had been no more than seven or eight yards away from us. One faint noise, and we should have been done for.

After an hour or two of sleep I awoke with the satisfied feeling of one who has found the right approach and now merely needs to perfect its details. I arranged for another trench to be dug on the opposite side, at a point that gave me complete coverage of the ground close to the old woman's remains.

Before dusk we had already taken up our positions again. Mundo, armed with his bow, stood back to back with me, so that between us we covered the entire field of vision. This time he had come along grudgingly, and made no bones about his distrust of my methods. Perhaps it is in this respect that we differ from savages. I had got up perfectly willing to modify my plan in some respects, while Mundo was incapable of learning anything from the previous night's mistakes. Since our ambush had not proved successful, he felt we should go back to the idea of a beat through the forest, as he and his ancestors had always done.

This time we did not have long to wait. It was little more than an hour before I felt a slight pressure on my thigh. I too had caught a slight rustle from the direction in which my gun was pointing. A moment later I glimpsed a gray shadow moving behind the thicket where we had lain the previous evening. I had never expected the creature to be so enormous. It circled the remains at its leisure, then slowly approached them, crouched down, and began to eat.

I held my fire, waiting for the best possible chance, anxious not to run the slightest risk of missing my target. There are few more lethal things in the world than a wounded jaguar. Finally I saw the glint of its eyes, and pressed the trigger three times in quick succession. The gray shadow gave a great sideways leap and vanished. Mundo sprang up behind me, bow drawn and ready. Not a sound was to be heard from the direction in which the jaguar had taken off. Then the dogs all began to bark, and the men from the village came tumbling out with torches in their hands. A little way off, in the middle of the thicket, we found an enormous jaguar stretched out in the immobility of death.

There followed an orgy of singing, shouting, and dancing. The beast was slung from a pole by all four legs and carried to the village, where we received a tremendous welcome. The dancing continued around the corpse.

I retired to my hut, suffering from the usual sick reaction that came over me after killing any creature. A thoughtful gesture of gratitude on the part of the village headman, later that evening, successfully eliminated my nervous tension, however. I was lying stretched out on the matting, unable to sleep, when a young woman slipped in through the doorway and stood waiting beside me. She was one of the headman's four wives, and he had assigned her, according to local custom, to entertain the guest of honor. It was weeks since I had been to bed with a woman, and this one proved both passionate and accommodating. There was no question of her wanting to get it over in a hurry, either; she stayed with me till morning.

Soon after dawn Mundo called for me. Everyone else was already up. The jaguar had been strung up in the middle of the village threshing floor: he was certainly a magnificent specimen, over six feet long, with a tawny, black-striped pelt. Mundo, acting as interpreter, told the headman that I would like to keep the skin for myself.

On our way back I decided that the right time had come

NAZARETH COLLEGE LIBRARY

for me to ask Mundo to be allowed to stay on with them: I could hardly have a more favorable opportunity. He replied that he would personally escort me to a village of Brazilian miners, one week's march to the south. Plain obstinacy is always a disconcerting hazard; it requires a great deal of finesse and patience to overcome it. But once again I had luck on my side.

When we reached the village there were no signs of that excited rejoicing which normally greets the destruction of a man-eating jaguar. The only expression on people's faces was one of alarm and distress. Poor Antu, it turned out, had taken a turn for the worse, and now lay hovering between life and death. The medicine man stood on the threshold of his hut, uttering frenzied invocations to every quarter of the heavens. From the interior there came wails of suffering and despair.

Mundo hurried in to see him, and I was left there alone, biting my nails in impotent frustration. I might well still be able to do something for the boy, but a barrier of ignorance and superstition stood between us. Round and round the hut there whirled a procession of men bearing staves hung about with amulets—animals' teeth, fishbones, skulls; and the medicine man himself swayed like a tree in a gale, howling and brandishing his wand, beseeching Mauri, the Kindly One, to come down and enter the hut. His invocation went something like this:

> *Hear, O Mauri,*
> *Hearken, O All-Knowing One,*
> *Hearken to the lament of Antu!*
> *Come, most venerable Mauri,*
> *Oh come, Mauri, most venerable One,*
> *And drive Canaima forth from Antu's body,*
> *With thy fiery hands*
> *Drive Canaima forth from Antu's body!*

And the chorus ran:

> *Hear us, O Mauri,*
> *O Mauri, hear us!*

When this litany had been three times repeated, the medicine man, holding his wand aloft before him, marched into the dying boy's hut and remained there for several minutes. Then he reappeared and began the chant once more, a little louder, a little more mournfully. Each time he entered the hut he poked his wand (which presumably acted as a conductor for Mauri's spirit) between Antu's toes, setting the other end to his own ear, and thus offering Canaima an opportunity to escape from the invalid's body. During this operation the chanting and dancing went on outside. One after another the dancers succumbed to the sun's blazing heat and collapsed, exhausted, only to stagger to their feet again after the briefest of respites and resume their rhythmic, compulsive jerkings. It would have been a comic spectacle had not the blind faith of these savages invested the whole proceedings with a deeply pathetic air.

Finally Mundo, who had himself joined in the dancing, staggered back to his own hut and flung himself down, panting, on one of the mats.

"How is he?" I asked.

"He'll begin to get better soon," Mundo said. Clearly he believed it. Either he had faith in the medicine man's exorcisms, or else he preferred to convince himself of their efficacy rather than sit by helpless and await the worst.

"The medicine man didn't have much success with Kaicusé," I said. "He declared Kaicusé would never come back, didn't he?"

"Medicine man say, the ashes were not properly gathered up. Not all were gathered. This is why the beast returned."

"That may be so," I said. "That may explain Kaicusé. But your nephew is another matter. Only I can save him. I possess the white man's medicine that will cure his sickness."

As I said this I showed him an ampoule of penicillin solution.

"This can save him, Mundo. Speak to the medicine man. Tell him."

He still needed to consider the matter: it was some time before he finally made up his mind. Then he went out and was gone for quite a while. I raged against the stubborn respect for tradition that all these natives had, and which kept my hands tied in a crisis: every lost minute lessened the chances of saving Antu. It was almost dusk before Mundo returned.

"Come," he said resignedly.

It was indeed a near thing. The boy lay there on his matting, with nothing but an animal-skin over him. He was shivering convulsively. Lolomai knelt beside him, trying to make him swallow some small morsels of casabe. The medicine man's four wives were there, too. The medicine man himself had withdrawn to his personal hut in high dudgeon.

I pointed to Antu's mother, indicating that she should stay, and begged Mundo to get rid of the other women. Then I went to work. I took Antu's temperature and found it was over 105° F. I sent for my *chinchorro* and put him into it, having first wrapped him up in my woolen blanket. It was not a difficult diagnosis: the boy obviously had pneumonia. I gave him an initial injection of penicillin and also made him swallow some aspirin tablets.

We sat up with Antu all night: at regular intervals Lolomai would change the cold compress on his forehead. He sweated profusely, and his system responded to my treatment in the most remarkable way. From the way in which Lolomai carried out my orders I could tell she trusted me. Mundo was behind me, and I felt his eyes boring into the back of my neck throughout; Antu's mother crouched in a corner, weeping continuously.

At dawn the following day rumor reached us that the medicine man was organizing another of his tribal dances. Antu had fallen asleep, and it was absolutely essential for him not to be disturbed by the din this operation would involve. I asked Mundo to tell the medicine man that the spirit of the great Mauri had entered the body of his son and was driving Canaima out. By this device I managed to avert more noisy ritual taking place around the hut.

I had the hut thoroughly cleaned and scrubbed out, and asked for a fire to be lit on the square. Then I put a hunk of tapir's meat to boil in a caldron. After it had been cooking for four hours I drained off a good rich sustaining broth from the pot, and made the patient swallow it. This did not require much effort on my part: he had eaten nothing for three days, and was extremely weak.

I remained by Antu's side all that day and the following night. Lolomai nodded off from time to time: she was nearly dead from lack of sleep. When she awoke she would look at me in a bewildered way, and then her eyes would light up with an expression of gratitude. Antu's fever had dropped, and he slept peacefully. At dawn on the second day I went back to Mundo's hut and sank into a deep sleep. When I awoke, some hours later, I perceived Mundo himself stretched out beside me, dead to the world.

I went back to have a look at Antu, who half opened his eyes and smiled weakly when he saw me. Mauri had accomplished his miracle; the boy's tough constitution had done the rest. Mundo was deeply moved. When he appeared from his hut he remarked to me: "The medicine man wishes to perform a ceremonial thanksgiving to Mauri. He will also have to thank him for delivering us from Kaicusé, and for your own presence in our midst. It is my hope that you will never leave us."

So even this old Taurepán headman had his moments of sentimental weakness.

"I have given orders to build a new hut for you, beside my own," he went on.

"Thank you."

"You will need a wife, too, if you are going to stay here."

I said: "Lolomai would suit me very well."

Mundo was clearly put out by this. He would not meet my eye, and went off without saying a word in response. But though this first request of mine seemed to have fallen on barren ground, nevertheless my most serious obstacle was now overcome: the Taurepán tribe had accepted me.

Chapter 6

◆

HERE BE DIAMONDS

When the juice of the yuca, an essential ingredient for brewing *cachire*,* had fermented for the statutory five days, we went off on a fishing expedition. Antu, who was by now convalescent, came along with us. We took five canoes and paddled upstream till we reached the next rapids, which were not very large or difficult. The men got out some *barbasco* roots† that they had brought with them, and began to pound them up on a rock in midstream: the juice from these roots has an anaesthetizing effect on the fish. Then we let the current carry us back downstream to the village, where we disembarked and posted ourselves at a strategic point on the bank, armed with bows and arrows. To each arrow a long, thin piece of liana was attached, so that we could retrieve any fish we hit.

Almost at once the fish began to appear, floating belly uppermost on the surface; and the native archers dispatched them with lethal accuracy, hardly ever missing. Even Antu was a wonderfully good shot. I, on the other hand, still found it difficult even to handle my bow properly. We got a tremendous haul this way, and every fish weighed at least two or three pounds.

All the inhabitants of the village where we had killed the jaguar assembled for the feast, together with folk from another

* A favorite Indian drink, made by boiling crushed manioc roots.
† This name covers various different herbs and roots, all of which have toxic effects to a greater or lesser degree.

community in the neighborhood, of which I had no knowledge. Among the guests was Kalamai, the young woman who had spent the night after the jaguar's death in my company. She appeared to retain a lively memory of our encounter.

Like everyone else, I put on a palm-leaf skirt, which was tied around my waist with a length of liana. The Sapulí and Mundo had supplemented this attire with the shirts I had given them, worn loose outside. This ridiculous getup certainly marked them out from the general ruck of bare brown torsos, and in the long run, I had to confess, gave them an undeniable air of dignity.

A great silence fell on the assembled crowd as the medicine man slowly advanced to the center of the square, and everyone else formed a large circle around him. Then he raised his arms to heaven and gave thanks to the venerable and ancient Mauri, thrice-greatest of gods, creator of all things, who had deigned to hear his prayers and grant him a favorable response.

All the natives chorused at this point: "Thou hast heard us, O Mauri! Thou hast heard our prayers!"

Then the dancing began, this time a gay and relaxed affair: two steps forward, one back, and a pirouette ending in a sort of curtsy.

When the thanksgiving ceremony was over, Mundo conducted me into the middle of the ring where everyone could see me. Then he proclaimed that henceforth I was one of them, that I would live with the tribe, that I was free to come and go as I pleased, and that if ever I stood in need of succor all were bound to come to my aid.

At one side of the great threshing floor, on a series of huge palm leaves, the feast was spread out—fish and meat dishes, turtle eggs, roasted grubs, and fruit, together with huge wooden bowls of *cachire*. Everyone eagerly began to eat and drink. But I could not take my eyes off Lolomai. In her palm-leaf skirt she looked even more attractive than usual, and even when she was pirouetting to the quick rhythms of the dance her breasts remained firm and high. I realized that my advances were not likely to be rejected, and that if I was so inclined I could have her that very night, since all the men, Mundo and the Sapulí included, were fast becoming drunk. But I preferred to bide my time.

The fact was that I had fallen into a sort of torpor, as sometimes happens when one sleeps longer than is strictly necessary. I felt at one and the same time identified with and utterly remote from these intoxicated savages. What kept me away from Lolomai was not so much any sense of decency or good manners as a certainty so profound that it seemed to paralyze my will power. I managed to convince myself that there was no point in my so much as lifting a finger, since if anything was going to happen to me here, among these simple people, it would come, at the appropriate moment, without any conscious effort on my part. And that included Lolomai, the diamonds, the bitter price I was to pay for them, and the dusty taste of responsibility left in my mouth (though of this, at the time, I thought not at all)—the whole profit-and-loss account, pleasures balanced against reckonings, which every man has to face in one form or another.

Naturally I did my best to fight this feeling of apathy: one explanation I found for it was the *cachire* I had drunk. To combat it I tried to marshal all the good, solid, logical reasons and positive motives that made me choose to sit there like a statue, enjoying the evening air, and watching Lolomai as though she were a slim young willow instead of a bare-breasted girl. I had wanted her for several nights now. Why didn't I take her?

The custom of the Taurepán as regards women and marriage I found extremely reassuring. No one would dare to touch a girl who was eligible for a husband, and since any man could take himself four wives, every girl automatically became a potential bride. Any man who flouted this law was exiled from the tribe and condemned to wander through the forest without food or weapons. His chances of survival were extremely slender.

Equally rigorous was the law concerning adultery. A husband had the right of life and death over his wife, and very few chose to be merciful over infidelity. The wretched woman's body was burned, and her ashes scattered in the river. On the other hand it was a great honor for a wife to be delegated by her husband to warm some distinguished guest's bed.

Women got married when they were about nine or ten, and if they had sisters these too became wives of the eldest one's husband, and moved into his hut. Sometimes a bride's sisters were mere infants, and on more than one occasion I heard a man say, pointing to some tot of two or three: "She my wife. Me bring her up."

If a bride had more than three sisters (which meant that the total number exceeded the legal maximum of four) those over and above the quota remained in their father's house. If on the other hand she was an only child, or had less than three sisters, the husband was entitled to take any girls subsequently born to his in-laws.

Women did all the work apart from fishing, hunting, and housebuilding. They went out in search of fruit, did the cooking, smoked the meat, deloused their husbands, and were responsible for removing from the soles of their feet, and under their toenails, certain small tropical fleas called *niguas,* which were fond of laying their eggs subcutaneously. But this latter chore was, in the event, seldom required, since the Indians had tough, horny feet, as impenetrable for the most part as a well-calked boat.

Finally, they were responsible for cutting their husbands' hair, which they did with a special sort of leaf that had a razor-sharp edge, chopping it off all around till it formed a sort of helmet. Shaving presented no problem, since the Taurepán, in common with most indigenous races of tropical America, are totally beardless.

There was no real jealousy or resentment among the women, though they were by no means strangers to the tantrums, backbiting, and fits of depression that we associate with jealousy. All of them, however, were convinced that they were mere chattels, lacking in all free will or purpose of their own. Since they married so young they were mothers by the time they were eleven or twelve, and, as one might expect, past their prime at twenty.

They had also discovered a certain plant that guaranteed them painless childbirth. When a Taurepán woman went into labor, her friends would gather the leaves of a herb that they call *mekurá*, pound them to shreds, and leave them on the boil for about three hours in a large caldron full of water. The resultant liquor was given to the expectant mother, who sipped it down a little at a time, and duly had her baby without feeling any discomfort. There was another root that they ground up in a makeshift mortar and boiled the same way for the purpose of producing sterility. A woman who was anxious to have no more children took two small doses of this decoction every day. The effect was to render her sterile for a period of two years. At the end of that time she could, if she so wished, do it again.

They all gave birth in the squatting position, beside the fire, with one or two other women assisting them. A couple of hours later they would calmly resume the task they had interrupted. During a birth the husband used to disappear into the forest, where, so I was told, he would suffer much pain himself. But since all witnesses were jealously excluded from this *couvade*-like retreat, I was never able to observe the process in action.

During this period I developed a close friendship with Antu, who often used to come around and visit me in the hut that had been built and put at my disposal. It was beyond doubt one of the best-equipped homes in the entire village, complete with door, window, and even a bath. Antu gave me lessons in the Taurepán dialect, which I found comparatively easy to pick up on account of its small vocabulary. (One or two examples to satisfy the reader's curiosity: "mother" and "grandmother" are represented by the same word, *amai*, while *bapai*, similarly, means both "father" and "grandfather." *Wakö* = good; *teleai* = good-by, or *au revoir*; *lemong* = thicket or savannah; *konog* = rain; *tuna* = water; *yun* = moon; *parú* = river; *pana* = forest; *acicá* = come here; *onda* = mouth.) In return I taught Antu some Spanish, and our conversations soon became pretty fluent.

I found this life much to my taste: it offered not only an abundance of all one needed but also absolute freedom in which to enjoy it. Yet in my leisure I still could not forget the motives that had brought me where I was, and on more than one occasion I discussed my plans with Antu. A few days after the feast I also confided in Mundo and the medicine man, who granted me permission to take the boy with me on an expedition. This pleased me very much, since Antu was a tough, adventurous character, with sharp wits to match, who knew the forest and all its perils like the back of his hand. He had given me a young puppy as a present—its father had been killed in a fight with a jaguar—and I christened it Kaicusé. We decided to take it with us on our trip.

The day before our departure I felt the time had come to tell Antu that I very much wanted to marry his sister. I was nervous about his possible reaction to this proposal, but he greeted it with a welcoming smile. Since we intended to be away till the beginning of the rainy season, that is, for the next three months or so, I saddled him with the task of formally asking his father's permission on my behalf. If it was forthcoming, I would marry Lolomai on our return.

Antu did not keep me in suspense for long. He hurried off right away, and shortly afterward was back with the answer. Lolomai was willing, but his father wanted to sleep on the idea.

That evening Lolomai came around to my hut with a present of wild pineapples, which was her way of telling me that she now considered herself my woman. I took her in my arms. But I had to keep myself well under control, as Taurepán law—and Antu's presence—required.

Next morning, before the rest of the village was stirring, we set out on our journey.

The canoe moved out from the bank, swinging with the current. Dawn was breaking, and the air had a humid smell. Nothing broke the deep stillness of the forest except the sound of our paddles thrusting through the water. Just for a moment, the thought of myself aboard this frail craft, with one Indian

and a dog for company, and no experience at all of diamond
prospecting, struck me as utterly absurd. God alone knew
what I might be up against. But once again all such worries
were dispelled by an inexplicable upsurge of confidence. As
I rode along in my dancing cockleshell, with the early light
lancing through the leaves and glittering on the surface of the
water, and no one to put my trust in but God, I rather fancy
the very precariousness of my position—nothing to lose and
my future in my own hands—filled my heart with unreasonable
courage. I looked around me and felt myself monarch of all
I surveyed.

What with my being sunk in such thoughts as these and
Antu's concentrating his attention on the current, we traveled
a good way without exchanging a single word. The sun was
already high in the heavens by the time we reached the
juncture of the Uai-parú with a small tributary. Here we
disembarked and unloaded the canoe. Next, we immediately
set about building a rudimentary hut out of broad palm leaves,
a simple *tarimba*, in which we had room to sling our hammocks and store our provisions and tools. Then I went off in
search of those close-packed stretches of gravel known to
prospectors as "diamond-bearing formations," and came upon
three of them. I decided to concentrate, to begin with, on the
one farthest upstream.

The first step in the operation is to divert the stream and
drain the area under scrutiny. Any sand and other detritus
covering the formation must be removed, and its hard outer
crust broken up. This upper layer of gravel must then be
shoveled away, till you reach the deepest stratum of all. Every
shovelful has to be passed through the *suruca*, the triple sieve.
When the top sieve is full you immerse the *suruca* in water
and set about the process of washing the gravel, moving the
suruca sideways and up and down alternately. The center of
the sieve is slightly concave, and any diamonds there may
be will collect in it.

The uppermost riddle has a coarse mesh, and sorts out
stones of three carats and over; the middle one catches those
of one carat or more, while the bottom one collects sand and

gold dust. To pick up the latter one requires yet another instrument, known as a *batea*, a wooden basin about eighteen inches in diameter, tapering to a conical bottom. But gold prospecting was not included in my program.

During this first washing stint we sieved about a cubic yard of gravel, and when we knocked off on the evening of our second day there all we had found were some paltry specks of gold: not the slightest hint of a diamond. Antu, who had no very clear idea of what prospecting entailed, was sadly mortified by this setback; it was as though he personally had been responsible for it.

The next day we moved on and tackled the second formation, quite close to the mouth of the stream. We worked here till late afternoon, but without anything to show for our labors. However much I told myself that such initial disappointments were without significance, I was beginning by now to feel a little uneasy myself. But once again events were to convince me that optimism has its uses.

The moment when I saw the gleam of my first diamond is not one I shall easily forget. I think I shouted aloud in my excitement. It lay glittering in the middle of the second sieve, a fine diamond of about two carats. So I *had* picked the right spot, after all! Carried away with enthusiasm, I embraced Antu, who beamed contentedly. To complete the picture Kaicusé began to scamper around us, jumping up and barking wildly. I turned the stone this way and that in my fingers, trying to stifle the vague sensation of foreboding that filtered into my triumphant excitement. I had thrust my hand into the bowels of the earth and plucked forth something that had lain hidden there since time immemorial. In the end the joy of acquisition was stronger than all other feelings; so much so, indeed, that I could not think of a safe enough hiding place for the gem, though I knew quite well there was no one there to rob me of it.

Before that evening four more smaller diamonds turned up in the fine-meshed sieve.

That night I found it difficult to get to sleep. When morning came I sallied forth from the hut bright and early, eager to

get to work once more. I happened to glance up and saw
something resembling a black cloud or swarm in the fork
of a tree. I looked more closely and perceived that it was a
cluster of apes, a regular family group, with father and mother
entwined together, holding their young ones beside them. I
stared, incredulous. Then, quite suddenly, they woke up,
untangled themselves from one another, and began to skip
chattering through the branches. The noise they made acted
as a sort of alarm clock for all the other apes in the neighborhood: a moment later the whole lot of them were howling in
chorus.

Antu had got up earlier than I, and now appeared carrying
a large fish, transfixed with an arrow and still wriggling. There
are some sights that occasionally leave me reflecting that a
man might profitably spend a good life just looking at them.

By the end of that day another dozen or so small diamonds
had accumulated in the bottom sieve. We spent four days in
all working this first stream, and then on the morning of the
fifth we re-embarked and traveled on till we found another,
which had only a poor trickle of water in it but was rich in
diamond-bearing formations. I therefore decided to make my
trial digs as close as possible to the infrequent pools (these
being indispensable for washing) which here occurred at
intervals of about two hundred yards.

The first day we found little of value. On the second, while
we were busy breaking up the outer crust in a formation, we
noticed the dog displaying signs of uneasiness. We looked
in the same direction as he was facing, straining our ears to
catch the slightest sound. The dog crawled between my legs,
coat bristling, and began to whine. Antu strung his great hunting bow.

"Kaicusé," he said.

In a flash I grabbed my rifle. There was a rapid patter of
feet and much crashing in the undergrowth. Ten yards away
from us two tapirs broke cover and darted away in the direction of the river. Then, about twenty yards behind them, and
in hot pursuit, came a pair of jaguars. None of the animals
noticed our presence. The one chance the tapirs had was to

get into the water, Then, instinctively, the dog charged off after the jaguars. Without thinking we began to run, too.

There came a thud and a screech of pain, and we quickened our pace. About twenty yards from the river we came on the two great cats, their fangs sunk deep in the throat and back of one of the tapirs. Blood was pumping out of the victim in great floods, and the female jaguar's muzzle and teeth were all dabbled red with it. It was she who first became aware of our presence. She dropped her prey, panting and snarling.

I hesitated an instant before I fired, caught by that instinctive distaste for killing which I have never managed to overcome. But Antu's arrow sang through the air, straight for the great beast's head; and in the same split second the jaguar twisted sideways, so that the shaft buried itself in her shoulder. She gave a roar of pain, and her mate crouched back, preparing to spring on us; but my bullet smashed into him before he could move, killing him instantly.

The female writhed and rolled over in agony, trying to free herself from the arrow that still quivered in her flesh. Then she flew at us, and we saw her in midair, all four feet off the ground, and both fired simultaneously. She fell at our feet, still jerking in her death agony.

Antu, who regarded these creatures as the most deadly enemies of his race, was jubilant; but I could not bring myself to share his pride so wholeheartedly.

That day we set aside our diamond prospecting and instead devoted ourselves to quartering the tapir and smoking its most tasty joints over the fire. We also rendered down a stock of its lard to serve as flavoring. This done, we moved on from the stream (which we christened Jaguar Brook) and continued our exploration of the river.

Day by day I felt myself acquiring a keener sense of hearing, touch, and direction—all qualities that anyone must possess in the jungle if he is to cope with the struggle for survival. Where the only law is that of victory to the strongest, the weak must needs fall back on craftiness and deceit, the ability to camouflage themselves and elude the aggressor. Slowly there awoke in me a primitive instinct for using every advantage, however tiny: I learned always to be ready either to defend myself or to attack others, and thanks to some ancient and mysterious sixth sense I could sense danger before it struck. At first I was obsessed, in a horrified way, by the constant echoing of the death screams of beasts attacked; but later I became used to the idea that this was an unending struggle in which no quarter was given, and where very often to kill was a necessary condition of self-preservation. The beasts of the forest breed and perish at a vertiginous rate. Ocelot, hawk, and snake between them account for literally thousands of rats. Panther, leopard, jaguar, and serval wage ceaseless war on wild boar, roebuck, tapir, and *lapa*. Ant bears gobble up ants by the million, bats gorge whole armies of insects, while their larger vampire cousins suck the blood of panther or jaguar cubs, weakening them and causing their premature death in many cases. The same process goes on in the aquatic kingdom.

I should never have managed to come out of that hell alive without Antu's help. It was not only his experience and advice and practical aid, of prime importance though these were: I also needed the inner comfort that the presence there of a fellow human being gave me.

So the three months passed, and together we learned something of the art of diamond prospecting. We found some in almost every dig, and on both sides of the main river.

Our stock of casabe was nearly exhausted, but we eked it out well enough with breadfruit. We made an excellent seasoning by mixing animal lard with a certain kind of red pepper (*aji*) which we had brought along in large quantities for that purpose. It is used in the preparation of a sauce that the Venezuelans call *guacasaca*, which goes admirably with meat. We ate a great deal of fish and woodcock. We lost weight, it is true, but felt as strong as lions. Even Kaicusé grew bigger: he was now all muscle and energy.

We pressed on upriver, till one morning we found ourselves facing a high precipice, with a cave at its foot from which the river debouched. This rocky barrier looked as though it was set there expressly to prevent us from going any farther: I felt a curious uneasiness at the sight of it. But to my suggestion that we might be well advised to turn back Antu replied that we still had a month to go before the rainy season, and it would be silly to waste it. He was, of course, quite right.

Ordinarily we built our hut as soon as our new prospecting site had been settled. This time, however, we spent some time looking around the place in a curious state of indecision. Even the dog wandered uneasily from one side to the other, then stopped and looked up at us with an interrogative air. Our eyes kept turning back persistently to that steep bluff ahead of us. It was an odd affair, bare of trees but rank with tropical vegetation and a mass of bright flowers, for all the world like a huge speckled pincushion dropped in our path.

To dispel this dangerous feeling of panic I walked across to the mouth of the cave from which the water poured out. The entrance was low, and we had to stoop down to get inside. After a little the roof got a bit higher, but still not high enough to let us stand upright. A few yards farther on it began to get steadily lower again, and we could advance no farther.

There was a sound of barking from outside, and Kaicusé came bounding in to make sure we were still there. He then dashed out and began barking again. When our eyes had accustomed themselves to the half-light, we looked down into the limpid water at our feet and perceived a bottom of ribbed and glittering sand. To probe this on the spot was one further way of breaking the magic spell that the whole place seemed to exert. We had hardly begun washing the gravel when I saw something shine through the contents of the top sieve. It was a diamond, all right, and the first one that had been big enough for the largest mesh to catch: a thirty-six-carat beauty.

I at once thanked God for His goodness. One's feelings at the time of a really important find such as this are always extremely confused: there are so many contradictory impulses thronging one's mind. I had often heard it said, too, that when a diamond of really outstanding size is discovered, something out of the ordinary always happens soon afterward. In point of fact I felt preoccupied and worried, and my thoughts kept drifting back to the village. But this formation was far too tempting to abandon, and in the last resort I could not tear myself away from it.

By early evening the hut was ready, and we spent four days washing the gravel in the cave. Then we shifted our attentions to a small nearby stream. Beginning at its mouth, we took up a cubic yard of its bed every two hundred yards or so. Finally we reached its source, which lay close to the ridge of the watershed. Down the farther slope we found a second stream, which joined the river before it vanished under the hill en route for the cave that we had already explored.

Since the first stream had produced a generous yield, it was well worth while probing the bed of the second one, too. We left the hut early in the morning, and did not get back till evening. It was a backbreaking task, but since we were soon due to get back to the village we could not waste time building a new shelter. As future chief, Antu had the welfare of the tribe at heart and wanted to be home a little before the rains broke: there were roofs that needed repairing, and they could do with an extra pair of hands for getting in stores.

So when we had finished washing this final formation we decided to pack up for the return journey. Normally we lit a fire at night to keep nocturnal prowlers away; but for once we felt too exhausted to collect leaves and sticks and go through the tedious business of getting them alight. We had a quick dip in the river, ate the fish we had prepared earlier in the day, and went straight to bed. The dog settled down between my hammock and the entrance to the hut. He was to pay dearly for his imprudence.

We got down to the river bright and early to begin the day's sifting. It was only when we were actually in the water that we realized Kaicusé had vanished. We called him repeatedly, but without result. Then we went back to the hut. It was Antu who first spotted the tracks of two big cats outside, and by studying them we saw that the female (who left shallower imprints) had paused a yard or two away, while her mate advanced to the threshold of the hut, broke poor

Kaicusé's spine with one quick swipe of his paw, and carried him off without making the slightest sound. Even Antu, whose hearing was extremely acute, had failed to detect anything at the time.

We followed the tracks and found our poor dog beside the river, half eaten and buried in sand.

Antu knew very well what sort of cat had done this, but could not convey this information to me, since his rudimentary tribal vocabulary had only a generic name for all of them. However, we both instantly decided, without a word being exchanged, just what it was we must do. About twenty yards away from the remains of the dog there stood a big tree. We quickly put together a sort of makeshift platform, and hauled it up to a point at which the main trunk spread out into three thick branches. We fixed it in this triple fork, and then camouflaged it with leaves and brushwood so that we could watch unobserved.

When evening came we climbed up into the tree, armed respectively with rifle and bow. We had before us the prospect of spending several hours at least in complete silence and immobility: any time between dusk and dawn might see our quarry appear, and the least whisper or rustle could scare them off.

Antu sat clasping the rifle. I had little confidence in his ability as a marksman, but he had insisted on having the gun: he wanted to exact personal revenge for Kaicusé's death. Yet in point of fact whenever I had let him take a shot he had hit the target, and I could only hope and pray that he would not miss it on so crucial an occasion as this.

Time crawled by: it seemed as though the night would last forever. Then the moon rose, and we had a clear view of the scene before us. At last there came a faint rustle in the undergrowth. We held our breath, muscles tensed. About twenty yards beyond the remains of the dog, the heads of two black panthers peered out from the undergrowth.

A few interminable seconds ticked by, and then the male advanced a foot or two, momentarily blocking our view of his companion. He took another cautious step, and then stopped, peering around to see if the coast was clear. Finally both of them padded over to the body of the dog. I had my heart in my mouth at this point, terrified lest Antu should miss the best moment to fire. But a second or so later the boy let fly, and his first shot took the male fair and square: it reared up on its hind legs and then rolled heavily over on its side. He fired again, almost immediately, and scored a hit on the female too, sending it toppling behind the body of its mate, without uttering a sound. To be on the safe side, Antu let her have a third shot. But the beast was craftier than we had anticipated. It seemed to recover itself suddenly, and with one tremendous bound disappeared into a nearby thicket. Instantly Antu fired again, straight through the quivering stems. There followed a total and decidedly reassuring silence.

We reloaded, and I had some trouble in preventing Antu from climbing down on the spot to get the situation under control. We passed the remainder of the night up on the platform, and only left the tree when dawn broke. The male panther lay there, his skull shattered. From the blood-soaked trail that his mate had left it was plain that she too was mortally wounded. We found her stretched out a hundred yards or so away, under a clump of bushes.

We buried the remains of the dog in the shade of the tall tree that had served us as a hide. Two hours later we were aboard the canoe, together with all our gear—including a pair of panther-skins, stretched out on two crossed bamboos.

Chapter 7

◆

LOLOMAI

We were traveling downstream, and the canoe skimmed rapidly along with the current: no need to paddle. Antu and I by now regarded each other as brothers, and conversed with casual intimacy. There was not the faintest shadow of rivalry between us, especially since Antu knew nothing whatsoever about the true value of diamonds. Indeed, every time we had found a stone he seemed genuinely jubilant on my behalf. At first these demonstrations of pleasure had left me surprised and not a little suspicious. But then I came to realize that the fact of my happiness was quite enough to set him off; and for my own part, I had always taken care not to let him know what significance these stones possessed in any civilized society. By so doing, I felt I would merely have unsettled— and to no good purpose—a simple mentality that was perfectly adapted to the life of forest and tribal community. Sometimes I told him stories about big European cities and the way of life there, and I could see in his eyes the eagerness to know more of such wonders. I talked about women with blonde hair and blue eyes, and he beamed in fascinated male complicity. He was a grown man already, and thinking of marriage. We agreed to have our weddings at the same time, immediately after the full moon, according to local custom. This made us all the more eager to get back.

It was delightful just drifting down with the current, under a thick shady canopy of leaves. Every twist and bend of the river recalled some episode in our long voyage of exploration. We passed quite close to the spot where we had both risked losing our lives, and which we had christened Snake Pool. This pool was about thirty feet wide and two yards deep; on our outward journey we had examined it and found it had a most promising gravel bottom. Antu had dived in with the canvas bucket and brought up a specimen load for sifting. It proved to contain one or two excellent diamonds, and it was certainly worth our while probing the site more thoroughly. We built a hut on the spot. But when Antu plunged in again to start the operation, I suddenly perceived a group of anacondas, each some thirty feet in length, wriggling out from beneath a large rock. Antu was under water, looking down at the bottom, and thus could not possibly have any idea of their presence. By now they were actually swimming directly above him. There was not a second to lose. I dived in, touched bottom, and, swimming under water the whole time, caught Antu by one arm and dragged him across to the far bank. The danger had been far from trifling, since these snakes are among the most deadly known to man. When we paddled the canoe out over the pool to recover our canvas bucket (we poked it up on the end of a long stick) the anacondas came writhing up to the surface and actually attacked us: we were forced to defend ourselves with machetes.

Farther downstream we passed by a stream that we had nicknamed Alma a Dios, since I had commended my soul to God there in the belief that my last hour had come. After a day's work I had gone down for a dip as usual. When I emerged from the water I noticed a trickle of blood running down my ankle. I paid little attention to it, and did not mention the incident to Antu. The next morning, however, my leg had swollen to twice its normal size. Antu had gone out early to catch some fish, and I lay there waiting for him in a great state of anxiety, praying God to spare me.

When Antu returned and saw my leg, he told me to lie still and not to worry. Then he disappeared into the jungle again. An hour later he was back with a bundle of red and green leaves, which he pounded up on a stone till they formed a sort of thick poultice. This he spread very carefully over my leg. Then he took a sharp stone and opened up the scab that had formed on my ankle, making it bleed again. He smeared the open wound with the leaf poultice too. The result was truly miraculous: the next day my leg had returned to its normal size.

As always happens when some danger is past and done with, we found ourselves laughing as we recalled the various details of these awkward situations. But we had in truth come perilously close to death, and if we laughed it was only out of relief at having had so narrow an escape.

We spent the first night of our return journey by what we called Fallen Tree Stream, where we found our original hut more or less intact. This name too commemorated a specific episode. I was in a pool some six feet deep, working a formation that had already, a short while before, yielded a diamond of more than five carats. Suddenly I heard a prolonged grinding, tearing sound. I looked up, just in time to see a huge tree toppling down over me. I dived down to the bottom of the pool, but when I tried to come up again I found myself trapped: the branches and leaves lay right across its mouth. All I could do was get my head above the surface. While I was trying to free myself, and turning my head in search of a possible loophole, I saw a water snake about a yard in front of my nose. Its two cold eyes were staring straight at me, and it was clearly ready to strike. I was petrified with terror. I dared not move an inch: if I went any nearer the creature I was done for. But Antu was on the lookout, and as soon as he spotted the snake he went for it, machete in hand, neatly chopping it into seven or eight separate pieces. Then, with considerable effort, he managed to release me from my highly uncomfortable position.

On the third day of the trip Antu suddenly steered the canoe ashore under the lee of the bank.

"*Báquiros*," he whispered.

His exceptionally keen ears had picked up the grunting of these wild pigs among the river selvedge. He was anxious to kill some in order to obtain a reserve of good meat for the tribe during the rainy season.

The wind was in the right direction. Antu studied the lie of the land for a moment, then waved me on after him. The herd numbered about a hundred, and it would have been a risky business getting too close to them. We stopped at something like two hundred yards' distance from the main body, where a pair of trees grew close together. Antu told me to climb up into one of them—he would take the other—and to hold my fire till he had loosed off his first arrow. The herd was certain to pass under us, he said. Sure enough, in a little while we saw them advancing through the bushes, and felt the earth shake as they surged forward. First came a sort of advance guard, and then, all on his own, the king of the herd, a fierce old boar. He paused some yards short of the two trees and sniffed the air suspiciously. Then, apparently reassured, he moved on once more. Close behind him came the sows and a clutter of young piglets, and the rear was brought up by the young boars, with their great curving yellow tusks. It was like a well-organized migration of human nomads, a whole nation on the move.

Antu's first arrow whistled through the air and transfixed one of the boars in the rear guard. The herd milled to a disorganized and panic-stricken halt. Then, at the sound of my rifle, they scattered frantically in all directions. The old boar went lumbering against the tide with desperate energy, nuzzling those that had fallen as though in an effort to succor them, helping the sows out of danger as best he could. But Antu's deadly marksmanship did not spare him, either. He fell with an arrow through his throat, uttering great squeals of rage and pain. I reloaded my rifle twice, and not a shot went wide. We had a fine haul of meat for the village indeed: between us we had slaughtered no less than fifteen pigs.

We came down from our trees, laid the pigs out in orderly rows, and hid them under a well-packed layer of palm leaves. Next day men from the tribe would paddle upriver and load them onto their bigger canoes.

After spending a night at Jaguar Brook, we decided to give

each other a good haircut before setting off once more. Antu was not what you would call a master barber, but the result was at least an improvement on the great shaggy mane each of us had grown during the past three months: a comic spectacle if ever there was one. I also shaved off my beard. We wanted to turn up in the village looking as two prospective bridegrooms should.

At last the first huts came in sight, and some women who were washing clothes by the river saw us, waved, and passed the news on to the rest of the tribe. By the time we disembarked everyone was there to meet us. Mundo had a smile for us both, and the old witch doctor did not lose the opportunity of thanking Mauri, in a loud voice, for bringing his son safely home again.

Lolomai stood somewhat apart from the others and waved to us cheerfully.

The whole tribe was a hive of activity, feverishly working to prepare against the onset of the rainy season and the specter of famine that accompanied it. During the four months of the *invierno* (the rains normally began in June, and sometimes lasted until October) the forest was quite impassable, and the continual downpour made fishing and hunting alike out of the question.

There was one big hut that served as a communal storehouse, and this already contained considerable supplies of casabe, together with smoked meat and fish. Against the walls stood orderly rows of gourds, filled with honey. Other provisions included fruit and red peppers. There were only a few days of respite left, and the men were now strengthening the roofs of the huts with additional layers of palm leaves and lashing up loose wall sections with lengths of liana.

Antu set to work and built a hut next door to mine, but of a very different sort from that normally found in a Taurepán community: he wanted to show how well he had assimilated the knowledge I had imparted to him during our trip together. He was going to marry Lometai, the daughter of Astru, who was headman of another village a little farther downriver.

Antu was exercising his undoubted marital privilege by taking to wife not only Lometai herself, but also her three sisters, the youngest of whom was three years old. Lometai herself was ten. The fact of his marrying four wives did not, of course, mean that he would at once have sexual relations with them all, including the youngest: each would await her turn. The natives were in the habit of justifying their polygamy on the grounds that it was essential for the preservation of the race; but in my opinion this explanation was simply one way of establishing a moral basis for the violent sexuality common to all those whose natural habitat is in the tropics.

The wedding ceremony had been fixed for the time of the full moon, and this was now only a few days ahead. It was vital that the preparations should be carried out with all possible speed, since once this lunar phase was past, no one could be married till another four months had elapsed. If on top of the tedium of the rains we were also doomed to physical continence, those four months would be worse than a stretch inside a monastery.

I was no less impatient than Antu: night after night I lay awake, stirred to feverish excitement by the way Lolomai looked at me, the promise of passionate fulfillment that shone in her eyes. She exercised the most profound fascination upon me; and a glance, a gesture, a tremor in the voice—anything that betrayed her instinctive desires—was enough to stir me into a state of violent longing.

Later, when I came to look back at this period, I was astonished at the way I felt not a twinge of nostalgia for the world I had left, no urge to return to my own people. Indeed, I behaved as though the rest of my life were to be spent here among the Taurepán, and I am sure that this mood of abandonment was in large part due to my passion for Lolomai.

At last the great day came. From midmorning onward guests began to stream in from the neighboring villages, all decked out for the ceremony in their palm-leaf skirts. The women brought presents—fruit, honey, a brace of wild fowl—which were put into a common pool for the great banquet. Our own contribution consisted of four of the wild pigs we had bagged on our homeward trip, which were now roasting on wooden spits, one at each corner of the square.

Such festive occasions were rare, and this one would certainly be the last before the rains set in. Everyone was determined to have a really good time, to eat, drink, and dance till they dropped from sheer exhaustion.

As soon as dusk fell all the villagers and guests gathered around Mundo—all, that is, but the two brides, who were making their own preparations and would appear only in time for the actual ceremony. A solemn silence fell as the Taurepán chief stood there in the glow of the firelight and declaimed the outstanding events of the tribe's history, from the far-distant past down to recent times. This was how the record of ancient glories and noble deeds, mighty hunters, mass migrations, struggles, and sufferings was handed down intact from father to son. Even I now formed part of their history: toward the close of his recital Mundo spoke of the warrior who had come from a far-distant land, and had been admitted to the tribe after wrestling with Canaima incarnate in the shape of a ferocious *kaicusé*.

When the moon was high the witch doctor arrived, hung about with all his bones and teeth and amulets and animals' tails, and marched out into the center of the square. Here he stood facing the hut from which Lolomai and Lometai, together with their mothers, would shortly appear, and began to chant some weird litany.

As our brides appeared, Antu and I went forward to meet them, took them by the hand, and advanced toward the witch doctor, who chanted louder the nearer we came, his recitative gradually turning into a sort of wordless ululation, a baying at the moon.

Two large straw baskets were now brought out, and into them the medicine man dropped a number of ants, which he shook out of a rolled-up leaf. Then, half naked as we were, the four of us were lifted up bodily by those performing the ceremony and made to sit inside the baskets, a helpless prey to the ants, which bit every part of us within range. Those excluded from this delicious feast began to swarm up our clothing toward our upper bodies. We were expected to bear this torture in silence for several minutes. It symbolized the adversities of life, which we and our wives would have to surmount together.

Then we were lifted out and given a little water by way of refreshment. The witch doctor's chant had now taken on a melancholy tone. I heard him pronounce our two names, and fancied that he was linking them with those of the gods in his native pantheon, entrusting us to their divine protection. Finally all the men, young and old alike, filed past the two girls, staring them straight in the face as they went. From that moment on Lolomai and Lometai were set apart, and no man except their husbands might approach them. When this procession was over, the Sapuli's chanting stopped too, and Mundo gave the word for the feasting to begin.

While everyone else set about the food and drink with a will, I took Lolomai by the hand and led her down to the river, where we tried to ease the pain of our ant-bites by dousing them in cold water. Then, clasping her close to me, I skirted around the edge of the village square, and together we entered my hut.

Chapter 8

♦

THE KADYUR

Three days after our wedding a sharp wind got up and sent vast black clouds scudding across the sky, heavy with rain, blotting out the sunlight. The treetops bowed down in a whirl of falling leaves, and the squalls whipped the surface of the river into a froth, till it came slapping over the banks. Dust storms swept across the village square, catching up wisps of straw, dry leaves, cinders, crumbling earth, and specks of grit in their turbulent, eddying course. A layer of grime settled on everything, so that the place looked even more poverty-stricken than it was. The *verano*—that is, the dry season, as opposed to the *invierno*, or rainy season, there being no change (naturally) of temperature—was now well and truly over.

Then, abruptly, the wind fell and there was a great stillness. While we were not expecting it yet the first flash of lightning forked down the sky, followed by a sharp, explosive burst of thunder. Flashes and thunder now followed each other in an ever-quickening crescendo, shaking the great forest trees, while the sky became heavier and more lowering from one minute to the next.

There was a bustle of activity in and around the village, with everyone doing something—putting away tools and utensils, hauling up the canoes and getting them under cover. In a very short time the river had become swollen and thick with mud, while leaves, brushwood, tree trunks, and dead animals went whirling downstream in the grip of the current. The level of the water was now some thirty feet above normal.

The odd satisfaction that we Europeans so often derive from a storm, the childish pleasure of taking shelter indoors, was in my case—and on this particular occasion—offset by a somewhat different reaction. The world of nature, which hitherto I had regarded as a rank, irrepressible force, and my deadly enemy, now suddenly revealed its kinship with me. Together we stood exposed to every danger, trusting in luck and the mercy of the elements.

The Indians accepted the change with their usual lack of emotional complication, and their equally characteristic unconcern. Even during these long months of enforced idleness, which heralded the oncoming winter, cheerfulness would keep breaking through. The women did the bare indispensable minimum of domestic work, just enough to keep things going, but no more. As for the men, they had one way, and one only, of passing their time. It was seldom that one passed a hut, by night or day, without hearing unmistakable noises— panting, creaking, and the like—going on inside.

In order to occupy my leisure I tried to introduce one or two innovations into these local customs. Unlike the natives, I was incapable of sitting still and doing nothing. I began to make brooms, and shelves for the storehouse, and ladders, and various other articles that I felt might be of general use to the community. I taught the men how to construct drums with the skins of animals. The idea proved a great success, and they all wanted one. I made up a dress for Lolomai from one of the panther-skins. It left one breast bare, but nevertheless she went prinking happily around in it before the entire tribe. I also taught her how to kiss, an art of which the Taurepán knew nothing, and which she found most enjoyable. Indeed, she developed an unbridled passion for this new thrill, kissing me on the lips whenever an opportunity presented itself.

Every day she became more fully a woman. When she caught me looking at her, she would blush deeply, and at once launch herself into my arms, clinging to me with arms and legs and hugging me tight around the neck. She would remain in this position till I picked her up bodily and carried her to our bed. Even then I had to take care not to leave her too soon, unless I wanted her to fly into a passion and scratch me. In a very short time she had become insatiable.

Love had transformed her, softening her features and taking the sharpness out of her normal expression. Her every gesture had softened correspondingly, and this, combined with the perfection of her figure, melted my physical longing into pure tenderness. As her desires were awakened, so was her sense of modesty. She would not go about naked any longer, but insisted on wearing a palm-leaf skirt. She had also begun to paint her face, with colors she obtained by chewing the leaves of certain herbs.

It rained continually, without the shortest respite, and yet life went on well enough. One evening I found myself wandering through the village at something of a loose end. For one reason or another, I forget exactly why, I had stopped outside the house of one of the witch doctor's wives, and it was abundantly clear that someone was busy making love inside. It seemed impossible to me that the aged Sapulí could still have the strength to play this kind of game, and so I went a little nearer, to make sure my ears had not deceived me. But no, I could distinctly hear the fast breathing of a man and the woman's moans of ecstasy. It simply couldn't be the witch doctor, I told myself. Yet this hut indisputably belonged to one of his wives, and he was the only man permitted to enter it. I put my ear close to the wall, only to receive ample confirmation of what I had previously suspected. The suspicion then dawned in my mind that despite the severity of the tribal laws, the witch doctor's wife was amusing herself with some young gallant. Consumed with curiosity, I concealed myself in the vicinity, determined to see just who the courageous fellow might be that was cuckolding my father-in-law in such fine style.

An hour elapsed, and throughout that time the sighs and groans continued without a pause. Finally someone appeared

on the threshold of the hut. It was, indeed, the witch doctor.
Holding himself erect, radiating energy, he strode purposefully
toward the hut of his second wife. I thought I must be seeing
things. I followed him discreetly, and listened. The sighs and
rhythmic movements began all over again.

Now I began to doubt the evidence of eyes and ears alike.
Was it possible that so wrinkled a veteran, who apparently
found even dancing too much for him nowadays, could perform so vigorously with one woman—for a good two hours,
moreover—and then start straight in again with another? This
seemed too much like magic to me—even for a magician.

I returned to my own hut absolutely flabbergasted, and
told Lolomai what was bothering me. She seemed astonished
that I should find it at all out of the ordinary. Obviously as
far as she was concerned this was a quite normal phenomenon.

I found it impossible to stick indoors with such a marathon
going on, and returned to my observation post. Shortly afterward I saw the witch doctor come out, and then make off
without delay in the direction of his third wife's hut.

I could hardly believe my eyes. I crept up after him and
managed to open a small crack between two of the palm leaves
in one wall. By the light of the central fire I could see the
old fellow bent over his third wife and riding her with
quite terrifying vigor. Monstrous shadows flickered across the
far wall.

By now I was convinced, willy-nilly, and I simply had to
find out what on earth the village made of this sex-fiend in
its midst. I went back to Lolomai, but could not convey to
her the sheer amazement (not untinged with admiration)
that the old boy's performance had aroused in me. Finally
I dropped off to sleep. When I awoke it was still dark, and
since Lolomai was sleeping peacefully still, I got out of bed
and silently padded along to the hut of the witch doctor's
third wife. All was still inside: he's finished at last, I told
myself, with a certain relief. But scarcely had this thought
crossed my mind when lo and behold, those all-too-familiar
noises started up once more, this time from the hut of the
Sapuli's fourth wife, which stood close by.

This time I made up my mind to stick it out and learn the full truth of the matter. I hid myself and waited patiently. It was not till dawn had broken that the witch doctor—drained, bent-shouldered, tottering on his feet—emerged from the hut and made his way to his own quarters in the middle of the enclosure. I allowed a few minutes to pass, then tiptoed across. He was snoring, which suggested that he had had enough for one night, at any rate.

For three days I kept a weather eye on the old wizard's hut, and watched the comings and going of his wives. It was only on the evening of the third day that he came out and was seen about the village again.

The whole business kept nagging at my mind, and I would have discussed it with Antu if the witch doctor had not been his father. In the end I turned to Mundo, who heard me out in great amusement and, when I had finished, remarked placidly: "Well, what's so surprising about that?"

The days passed. One afternoon I saw Zambo emerge from the hut of one wife and immediately pass on to that of another. Zambo was a mild, bleary old soul, who seemed close to death's door. The tribe regarded him as more or less pensioned off, and he spent his time weaving osier baskets. Without any effort to conceal what I was up to, I listened outside the hut, as close as I could get. No doubt about it: to cut a long story short, it was like the witch doctor all over again.

There must be a catch in it somewhere, I thought. There had to be. It was downright impossible for old men with one foot in the grave to perform like that for hours on end. Maybe I was on the brink of discovering something more valuable than all my diamonds.

I began to keep an eye on all the village elders. One evening it was Mundo's turn. I hurried off to rouse Antu, and dragged him along to the hut that his uncle had entered a short while before.

"What are they doing in there?" I asked him.

He listened carefully, grinned, and said, without any sign of discomposure: "Making love."

"Right," I said, scarcely able to control my excitement. "You know what'll happen now? Your uncle will come out of here, and move on to his second wife, and from there to his third and fourth. How on earth does he manage it?"

Antu began to laugh. He said: "Come on, let's get back to bed. I'll tell you all about it in the morning."

I insisted on being told the secret forthwith, and Antu finally gave in. We sat down together in his hut, and he told me the story of the kadyur.

Long, long ago there lived a man who had four wives and got on very well with them. But one day disaster struck. While the four wives were out in the forest gathering fruit, warriors from another tribe invaded the village, slaughtered the men, and carried off the women. The four wives thus found themselves all alone, and began to cry. While they were still bewailing their fate, up came a kadyur, which is a kind of large dog. The kadyur comforted them with smooth words, and said that if they would take *him* as their husband, he would hunt and fish for them. The women were so grateful that they began to stroke and caress him, whereupon the kadyur mounted all four of them in turn, without his energy slackening for a moment. He repeated this performance every day, and the women all became besotted with him.

But one fine morning their real husband turned up again. He had managed to escape being killed, and had wandered off into the forest. When he learned about the kadyur, he flew into a terrible righteous fury, and by way of revenge cut off the poor beast's genitals, to the great distress of the kadyur itself and, indeed, of his four wives.

The mutilated dog fled into the jungle; and the women, who could not resign themselves without a struggle to the thought of losing such a creature comfort, put the severed parts to dry out in the sun. When they were dry and ready, the women ground them up into a sort of flour, and put a pinch of it in their husband's dinner every day. Within a very short time the village was repopulated.

I could not understand the relevance of this story to the events I had witnessed, and said so.

"But the kadyur really exists," Antu explained.

During their last hunting trip, it seemed, the men of the tribe had succeeded in capturing a kadyur, and had promptly sliced off its genitals, distributing a small piece to each of the village elders. This was a perquisite reserved for them by ancient tradition. Once they had absorbed a bit of it, they could then enjoy themselves with their wives.

However, it appeared that the kadyur was well on the way to extinction, since countless generations had hunted it remorselessly. The most important thing was to catch it alive, too; otherwise its genitals might fail to procure the desired effect.

I saw Mundo again, alone, two days after this conversation. I told him I knew about the kadyur, and wanted to test its powers myself. He protested that at my age I had no need of aphrodisiacs, and that with only one wife I was in no position to conduct such an experiment. Then I attempted to persuade him that my natural curiosity was not the sole motive involved, and that I wanted to test this substance in order to find out whether it was worth while breeding kadyurs in captivity. He gazed at me in astonishment: such a notion had never entered his head. I managed to extract a promise from him that one day soon he would give me the opportunity I sought.

About a week after this the old medicine man died. No one shed a tear for him: these people accepted death with fatalistic resignation. His corpse was buried in the middle of his hut, and the hut itself burned. His four wives passed, by right of succession, to Antu, who was at once obliged to start building extra huts beside his own to house them. One of these widows was still a young woman, and Antu offered her to me.

"You have only one wife," he told me. "That can't possibly be enough."

I was a little doubtful about the idea. Polygamy was not a natural part of my mental or moral climate. I was not, to be sure, particularly bothered by the idea of going to bed with another woman, but I somehow could not get around to

the idea of having two wives. Also I was afraid of offending
Lolomai. This scrupulousness surprised Antu, who, like all
Taurepán males, regarded women as possessing absolutely no
rights or independent personality of their own. So more or
less involuntarily I found myself saddled with a second wife.
Lolomai took the news very well indeed, and welcomed her
new colleague most amiably. After all, she was the Number
One wife, and would always take first place. Her reaction was
diametrically opposed to mine: she accepted the principle, the
idea of polygamy as an institution, but would have been
furious if I had chosen to spend the night in her rival's hut.
As a result the only time I slept with Urulai was when I took
the kadyur potion.

Late one afternoon Mundo sent for me. He was sitting with
a small bowl of *cachire* in front of him, and nodded to me
to join him, without saying a word. With almost religious care
he then brought out his little piece of dried kadyur, as hard
now as any bone, and scraped away at its surface over the
bowl. A small dusty deposit fell into the cachire. Then he
replaced the kadyur in the pocket of his pants and stirred the
brew up a bit. We sat there for half an hour or so, chatting
and sipping this novel pick-me-up.

I imagined I would feel some effect—heaven knows what,
exactly—straight off; but by that evening there had been no
particular change in me that I could notice. Then I retired
to bed with Lolomai. Whether it was the dose I had taken
that worked me up so quickly I cannot be certain; but it was
beyond doubt on account of this aphrodisiac that it required
six or seven hours of the most agonizing tension (rather than
pleasure) before I finally achieved release.

In my nightly bouts with Lolomai I lasted, on the average,
about twenty minutes. That evening it was a very different
story. Mentally I was longing to reach a climax, and physically
I did my utmost to bring it about; but after three or four
hours, despite all my persistence, despite Lolomai's caresses,
despite my powerful imagination, I was still going strong, as
far from the end of the road as ever.

Lolomai knew about the drug I had taken, and was well

aware of its effect; but she had obviously hoped that I would be able to consummate my desire with her alone. In the event, however, the poor girl was absolutely exhausted; she gave up at last and implored me to stop. I must confess that to have rendered Lolomai *hors de combat,* even once, was the only real satisfaction I derived from this experiment.

So I left Lolomai to get some sleep, and went along to see my second wife, who knew what I had been up to, and was expecting me. Though she evinced mild surprise at my demands, for over two hours the poor girl did her utmost to please me in every way she knew.

When Urulai was done in as well—and she tired rather quicker, not being so young—I returned to Lolomai, who was sleeping the sleep of total exhaustion. After another hour, thank God, I attained my goal. I felt like death.

A day or two later old Zambo really did die on the job, in very similar circumstances. I found out then that the witch doctor had suffered the same fate.

I decided not to bother about the kadyur idea any more.

More than two months had now elapsed since the beginning of the rains. Every day, about the same time, the sky would become overcast with heavy clouds, and a stiff south wind got up. Squalls howled through the forest, and many trees were struck by lightning. The occasional lull in the storm was of short duration. While it lasted I could hear the cadenced drip of raindrops falling on the dead leaves that roofed my hut, repeating the leitmotif of what, surely, was the earliest music the world ever knew. Provisions began to run short; the fruit had been used up some while already, honey was reserved for the children, and I found the smoked meat and fish quite uneatable. This left casabe, and there was by no means too much of that.

Occasionally, driven by hunger, a group of men would sally forth on a brief hunting expedition, taking advantage of a temporary bright spell. But all they ever brought back was a parrot or two, which had flesh as tough as old leather. And to get even this meager bag they were obliged to struggle deep into the jungle, knee-deep in mud. Then, when they were hot and sweaty, down would come the rain again, and by the time they got back to the village they would be shivering with fever. Cases of pneumonia were frequent, and the new witch doctor had his work cut out to keep Canaima at bay: he danced and chanted for hours on end.

So long as I had any penicillin I could intervene myself, but even this ran out. From that time on pneumonia claimed an increasing number of victims. Taurepán medicine was primitive in the extreme, and consisted for the most part of plasters compounded from leaves and ashes (to slap on open wounds) or copious draughts of hot water and ventral massage (to assist women in labor). When a baby was born, they severed the umbilical cord with a wooden knife, while the placenta was wrapped in a big leaf and taken up to the top of a tree. No one could ever give me any explanation of this custom.

Their great panacea was fire, which they believed could cure everything, or almost everything. In the majority of cases a sick person simply dragged himself close to the flames and waited for Canaima to go out of his body. Only in really serious cases was the witch doctor called in, and then much as we would summon a priest to administer Extreme Unction to a dying patient.

I spent a great deal of time trying to work out some method whereby I could help the tribe to get through their winter in a less calamitous fashion. I had already tried to get one basic idea into Mundo's head—and, with even greater persistence, into Antu's, since he was younger and therefore more open to new suggestions: the idea of organizing ahead during the summer, and breeding animals in captivity. The trouble was that none of them had the faintest conception of what foresight meant. On top of that, they didn't know the meaning of hard work, either, and any suggestion I made which involved co-operative labor provoked either bewilderment or hilarity.

They were so lacking in initiative that none of them had ever bothered to work out a technique for fishing when the river was swollen and muddy on account of the rains. They just waited—waited until the water level sank again, and they could resume their only known methods of catching fish, with bow and arrow and *barbasco* root. The result of this was that for four good months of the year they either went hungry or ate half-rotten fish.

One day I found myself thinking of the fishing nets I had seen employed, during my childhood, in the rivers of Italy. They were not much larger than an ordinary bed sheet, stretched out over two crossed canes, and suspended by the four corners from the end of a long pole. I got hold of some lengths of liana, and at once set about making a net out of them. The natives, their curiosity aroused, stood watching me; some even tried to lend me a hand in their own clumsy fashion. By evening the net was finished, and early next morning, with Antu and four other men, I carried it down to a nearby stream. I tied a stone to each of its four corners, and put another heavier one inside it, together with a hunk of putrefying meat. Then I anchored the whole affair to the bottom. The water was so muddy that it was impossible to make out what was going on below the surface; but after a little while we observed tremors in the portion of the net still above water. On hauling it up we found four fish in it, each one a five-pounder or over. We spent the morning fishing in this way, and by midday we had caught enough to provide a good square meal for the entire village.

We fashioned two more nets from liana, with the prospect, next summer, of replacing them by more durable ones, for which we would employ a certain long, tough plant that could be woven into excellent cord. Meanwhile there would at least be no shortage of fish during the latter end of this winter, and I felt happy, for the children's sake if nothing else.

Apropos children, I had embarked upon a long and at times discouraging struggle to break the natives of the habit they had of keeping their children at the breast till they were three or four. If the mother's milk supply failed for any reason, the poor child was almost inevitably doomed. On more than one occasion I had to come to the rescue of some child in an advanced state of malnutrition, and feed it casabe pap. Finally, by a process of trial and error, they came to the conclusion that my method worked better than theirs, and decided to give in.

Though, as I have tried to indicate, I was by no means

short of occupations, I would nevertheless have died from sheer depression and boredom if it had not been for Lolomai and Urulai. They were both extremely affectionate creatures, who took tremendous pains to please me: the most tasty bits of our meager repasts were always reserved for my enjoyment. I had not laid a finger on Urulai since the memorable night of the kadyur, but now I was beginning to find her rather attractive. One evening, after supper, she rose as usual to retire to her own hut, but this time I caught her by the arm and made her stay. The poor girl was only too pleased to accede to my desires, but Lolomai intervened in a spitting fury, and it needed much finesse—both verbal and amatory—to soothe her down. I began to feel, in a rather desperate way, that I had made a ghastly error of tactics. But finally, and most unexpectedly, she agreed to let Urulai share our bed. Soon it became a regular habit for us to spend the night *à trois,* and even Lolomai professed herself pleased with the arrangement after a while.

But despite the extra diversion provided by Urulai, I knew, with ever-increasing certainty as time went on, that what I really needed was a European wife. It was not a necessity in the physical sense, but I thought about it constantly, for all that.

Our food supplies were now quite exhausted. Unless I managed to find some way of replenishing them, it seemed probable that the one hundred and twenty unfortunate members of this village community were doomed to die of starvation. I made several forays into the jungle with Antu, going more or less naked to avoid the consequences of wearing sodden clothes; but all signs of animal life seemed to have disappeared forever.

One morning, however, Mundo came around and woke me early. A man had turned up from the next village with the information that a horde of monkeys had been spotted in the forest, not very far off, either. If we could catch up with them before they moved on, we might have the answer to our food shortage.

It was a nightmare trek we made, Mundo and myself and every other able-bodied man in the tribe, through torrential rain, sinking knee-deep in mud at every step. The headman of the next village had sent off some men in pursuit of the monkeys, and after a couple of hours we heard them answering our shouts, with a whickering cry rather like that of a screech owl. We struggled on in the direction of the sound, and finally caught up with them. The monkeys, it appeared, had gone to ground: they disliked the rain as much as we did. Mundo threw a cordon around the area, and our beaters moved in for the kill.

Antu fired the first shot, and this was the prelude to a tremendous carnage which I shall never forget till my dying day. If I had had the remotest idea of just how ghastly a business it would be, I should never have gone on the expedition at all. Dozens of bowstrings twanged together, dozens of arrows sped inexorably to their mark. Through the hiss of the rain a chorus of agonized, semihuman screams rent the air, screams of rage and terror and pain. This frantic uproar was followed by a spectacle as pitiable as it was appalling. The males, enraged at their inability to halt the slaughter, beat their breasts and foreheads with hairy fists, howling horribly; while the females, their babies clinging to their backs, skipped from branch to branch, maddened with fright, trying to get away. But the merciless arrows brought them down; and when the wounded ones, eyes rolling, saw their assailants approach to finish them off with clubs, they began to scream for mercy, holding up their paws to protect their little ones. As the clubs rose and fell, ghastly squeals and piteous broken wailings continued down in the mud.

Their twisted, pain-racked features are still stamped indelibly on my memory: human faces they seemed, not animal, made ugly by the terror of death, twitching masks, eyes that begged and pleaded as human eyes might have done. The slaughter continued with such unbridled ferocity that it gave me the cold shivers. Exasperated by a two-hour slogging march through mud and torrential rain, driven on by gnawing hunger and (a more potent stimulus) their sudden collective blood lust, the natives shot and clubbed with frenetic abandon, till I was on the verge of intervening and stopping them.

But I did not do so. Once again, death to the one meant life for the other. It was a bloodier business than at any Italian slaughterhouse; but man has always been a killer, and death comes for him in the end too.

Finally the wretched creatures gave up all hope of escape, and crouched over the bodies of their little ones in a last attempt to protect them. The dogs, famished as they were, and aroused by the smell of blood, finished the job off with savage ferocity.

Then, at last, all was still. We took back forty-seven of these unlucky beasts for our village alone, including several females that had died still clutching their babies to them. We got home at dusk, aching in every limb, on top of which I felt sick with disgust as well. The women had already lit the fires for smoking all this meat, and promptly set about their task. That day's hunting kept famine at bay for the remainder of the year.

Every morning Mundo would look up at the northern sky; like Noah, he was expecting a sign. Antu, now in a thoroughly sanguine mood once more, began to talk about our next expedition to Kaicusé Mountain. He intended, this time, to take his wife along for the trip, and Lolomai insisted on accompanying us as well. My instinct was against this: I felt a flicker of anxiety deep inside me, a voice that declared I ought not to give in to her. But finally she managed to soften my heart, and I promised her she should come. Then it was Urulai's turn, but this was really out of the question and she had to resign herself to staying behind.

Finally the sign Mundo had been awaiting materialized, in the shape of a flight of birds passing southward over the village. Two days later the headmen of the other villages that lay to the north and south of us arrived for the general assembly held annually at the end of winter. Each in turn gave a brief account of the vicissitudes his people had endured in the past months, and then put forward his future projects for debate. Favorite subjects were the extension of yuca cultivation, a more equitable distribution of men in the various villages, and the proper way to prepare curare, the venom that the Taurepán daub on their arrowheads. This process demanded the sacrifice of a human life, and traditionally the lot used to fall on the oldest woman in the three villages. The poor creature knew she had to die; it was a tribal custom that had been observed since time immemorial. No one ever thought of rebelling against the decree, and at least they had a painless end. The old woman's task was to keep stirring the roots while they boiled, for a day and a night. The poisonous fumes rising from the pot during this process of decoction killed her slowly, without her really being aware of what was happening. That particular year the lot fell on a woman in the village up north, which meant, somewhat to my annoyance, that I could not observe the preliminaries: I had hoped to see exactly what roots they employed.

Soon after the assembly was over a wind got up which blew the last of the clouds away. The sky was blue once more, and for the first time in months the stars could be seen at night. With astonishing speed plants and flowers began to come up again in rank profusion, while the forest echoed to the clamor of troupials, wild duck, and *gonzalitos;* and in a few days the river was back to its old shade of indigo once more.

It was time we began thinking about our expedition.

The first thing we needed to do was to repair the canoe we had used the previous year and build a second to go with it. The old one was a strong, heavy craft, which could easily carry the gear and provisions as well as Antu and myself. The new one we decided to construct from light bark, and allot to the two women and the dog. At the same time there was matting to be woven for coverlets and mattresses, and supplies of rope —both from the same raw material.

I spent the night prior to our departure with Urulai, turning a deaf ear to Lolomai's protests. When morning came my second wife was down at the river to see me off. Tears were running down her face, and she did not wait to see my canoe move out from the bank into midstream, the final moment of departure.

Chapter 9

◆

FROM A VIEW TO A DEATH

It was a fine clear morning. The sun's rays glowed behind the jagged mountain ridge, climbing slowly up the sky to illuminate forest, village, and riverbank. The whole tribe had gathered to watch our departure, and we waved back at them till we were around the first bend, and the dense foliage hid them from our sight.

Lolomai and Lometai were such skillful canoeists that very often they forged ahead of us, and when this happened they would shriek with delight. We found the river very much changed; at one or two points the winter flooding had been so violent that the channel had shifted its course. Some of the little islands had vanished, and fresh ones had appeared. The current had swept away all the huts we had built the year before, and huge ceiba trees—the *bombacacea,* or kapok tree, of very light wood—had fallen across the river in places, spanning both banks.

It took us a week to reach Kaicusé Mountain, but we had a most pleasant trip. As soon as we felt tired we called it a day, and spent the rest of the afternoon swimming. All the time I became increasingly aware of the same marvelous feeling of freedom I had experienced the previous time, but now it gave me even deeper pleasure.

We spent the seventh night after our departure at the same spot where poor Kaicusé had been attacked by the panther. I was anxious to get on. The next morning we humped all our gear over the "mountain" by hand. As the reader will have gathered, it was not a real mountain so much as a hill, some nine hundred feet high, and thickly covered with vegetation. We had decided to make this point the base for all further exploration, so we took more than usual care over the construction of the hut, even equipping it with a good solid door that could be shut fast at night.

Three days later Antu and I set off together. The girls had their small bows to defend themselves with, and we also left them the dog. We abandoned the small stream and turned instead to the main river, making a trial sounding every two hundred yards or so, but without result. We crossed over to the left-hand bank and tested a tributary that we had noticed there. But still no good. We found not a single scrap of evidence to suggest the presence here of either gold or diamonds. Every dig we made in this area gave the same negative result.

Since every stream on the other side of the hill had yielded diamonds—not to mention the main river in the cave and lower down—it seemed clear to me that the hill itself was where they must come from.

Before we finally gave up, however, I wanted to check the validity of my argument a little more thoroughly; so we pressed on upstream for a while, searching and exploring, but without success. At this point I felt that my theory had been amply confirmed; so we turned the canoe around and returned to base.

It was only a few days since we had left the women, but hardly were we back before Antu—following the custom of his people—fell on Lometai, and the two of them got down to it there in front of us. Lolomai, who was standing at my side, had learned to avoid such extremes of public effusiveness. During our absence she had found a secluded spot where the stream formed a small pool, nine or ten feet deep in the middle, and flanked by a narrow strip of white sand. Lolomai had smoothed out a patch a couple of yards long under a tall, shady palm tree, hedged it in with bushes, and spread out some matting in it in lieu of a bed. It was an ideally peaceful place, and she took me off there as soon as I got back, so that we could put it to its intended use without delay.

The next morning, while working the stretch of river between the stream and the mouth of the cave, we found some diamonds. Now I was absolutely convinced that the "mountain" was the prime source of these stones, and I became impatient to explore it more thoroughly. We discovered that it was not one huge rock, but a pile of boulders, some of them enormously large. They had a consistency resembling that of granite, and must have been formed by some primeval cataclysm that exploded them skyward, after which they fell back in the tumbled heap that we now saw. There were plenty of holes and cracks between one rock and the next, and once we had cleared away the dense growth of aralias, asparagus, ficus elastica, and philodendron that blocked their apertures, we might well find a possible entrance. However, these fissures and passages were inhabited by an assortment of snakes, owls, and bats. Despite the hazards I managed to take several samples of earth from them, and washing revealed, in each case, gold dust and fragments of quartz.

One day we managed to wriggle some thirty feet into one of these holes, and could distinctly hear the muffled roar of a waterfall. We were on the southern side of the mountain, the same side, that is, as our base hut. I felt it might be an idea to take a bearing from the north side as well, through the cave that carried the river—and where we had found our first really big diamond on the previous trip.

We penetrated about twenty yards into the grotto, till our heads were barely above water level and we could get no farther. The sound of the waterfall was audible from here, too. It became plain that it must be located somewhere in the very heart of the mountain. Such cascades always form hollow pools that collect matter carried downstream. During the rainy season the lighter flotsam gets swept away by the swollen current, but heavier stuff—such as gold and diamonds—sinks to the bottom and stays there.

This mountain had probably stood here for several millennia, and every day some particle of rock containing gold or diamonds had broken loose and come drifting downriver. No one had ever penetrated to that pool in the center of the mountain: by now it must be a sort of vast natural treasure chest. The diamond fever was on me again, and I could hardly wait to get my hands on the stuff.

The only method we could clear a way for ourselves was by burning out the local fauna, for a start. So with the help of the women we cut away the undergrowth from all the apertures on the hillside that looked big enough to crawl through, stuffed them with sticks and dried grass, and set fire to the lot of them. Then we sat back and waited. For two days the mountain belched smoke, and when we went and had a look we found that the snakes and owls had moved to other lodgings. It was now that the hardest and most dangerous work of my entire expedition began.

Antu, who had absolute blind faith in my judgment, followed me without turning a hair. We tried every possible entrance passage: sometimes we managed to get about twenty or thirty feet in, but there was always some unexpected obstacle that brought us up short and sent us out again, bleeding, bruised, bitterly disappointed, and moving backward because there was no room to turn.

After several days of these abortive attempts, I was almost on the point of chucking up the whole idea. The exhaustion produced by crawling along dozens of tunnels seemed to have killed any zeal I originally might have had to find my Open Sesame. I got to the point where I was furious with myself for having wasted so much valuable time to no purpose. I was on my way back to the hut, tired and dejected, when Lolomai came running to meet me, waving her arms in excitement, saying that she had found an opening, close to a palm tree, from which the noise I sought was plainly audible. It was almost at the very top of the mountain. Next morning we examined it—an irregular aperture, but quite big enough to let a man through comfortably. I cleared away the vegetation that sprouted from it, and put my head inside: the roar of the waterfall was clear and distinct. I reckoned I must be about forty yards above the subterranean river channel, and in all likelihood right over the waterfall itself. It struck me as odd now that I had persisted in searching around the lower hillside, and never thought of looking for a vertical shaft.

I lobbed a stone down. I heard it hit solid rock with a momentary clatter, but there was no sound of a splash. I tried with a bigger stone, but just the same thing happened. Then I tore off a long branch from a tree and pushed it straight down the hole for about twenty-five feet, at which point I felt it touch ground. By moving it delicately around I discovered that this was where the shaft changed direction, in a sort of elbow bend. Without another moment's hesitation I decided to go down the hole myself, buoyed up by the familiar sensation of frenzied excitement which—only that morning—I had been convinced I would never experience again.

I knotted two lengths of liana rope together, and anchored one end around the trunk of the palm tree that stood close by. As I descended, Antu paid the rope out, very cautiously. All I took with me was a long stick with which to feel out the ground ahead of me and judge the size of the passage. I am not ashamed to admit that my heart was in my throat all the way down.

After a descent of about thirty feet I touched ground. Squatting down, I could just make out, by the faint light that filtered down from above, the somewhat shallower incline of the tunnel's continuation. I tied the liana rope around my waist and slowly moved forward down it, feet first, more or less on my back. The light dwindled as I went on, and soon it was quite dark. Every two or three feet I would stop and use the stick to probe the ground ahead of me, and judge the height of the roof. Then I would resume my inch-by-inch progress again, with back and buttocks as my main source of motion. The passage was so narrow that I scarcely had elbow room. The darkness and cramped conditions between them had an unpleasantly oppressive effect on me. As a result I suddenly recalled that we had not fumigated this part of the mountain, and that I was therefore quite liable to be attacked by a snake or some other reptile. I was in about the worst situation imaginable for holding out against the inroads of natural fear:

cut off in the dark, I saw myself as virtually defenseless. I had moments of frightful uncertainty, wondering whether to press on or go back and burn bundles of grass in the mouth of the shaft to drive the snakes away. Perhaps I was merely casting around for some excuse to get out into the open again and pull myself together. But while these thoughts were passing through my head I went on wriggling my elbows, arching my back, and pushing my legs forward, more or less mechanically. After a while I realized that my arms were no longer pinned in by the side walls, and felt more myself again. By thrusting the pole upward I found I had enough room to stand on my feet. At first I nearly lost my balance in the darkness, but as soon as I had steadied myself I made another attempt to touch the roof—the pole was some eighteen feet long—and found I could not do so. I waved the pole around my head and encountered no obstacles. Clearly I was in some sort of large grotto.

I took about ten steps forward, and then probed with the pole again. This time I found a rock face in front of me, and went closer till I could touch it. It was rock all right, a blind wall of rock that formed the end of the cave. Yet from somewhere quite near I could still hear the sound of that waterfall. I continued my tour of investigation, feeling with my toe before every step I took, pointing the pole ahead of me or rotating it behind my back. Because I could not see I felt in some curious way that I was unable to trust my ears, either. It was only when I was right on top of it that I became aware of another tunnel, from which there issued an icy draft of air—and the sound of rushing water.

I wriggled into this new passage on my back, as before. After something like thirty feet—though at the time it seemed a much longer distance—the tip of the pole wavered up and down without encountering any solid object. I was now doubly cautious over my every movement; and soon, sure enough, I found my legs dangling in the void. By the feeble light that filtered in through a small crack overhead a cavern of positively Dantean characteristics was revealed to me. Behind a cloud of spray the water fell, directly in front of me, for about eighteen or twenty feet, ending up in a pool some ten yards across. From here it was sucked down into a vast cavern nearly forty feet below where I was perched. The walls of this funnel were composed of massive blocks similar to those that formed the outer shell of the mountain, and so clumsily piled up that they looked on the point of collapsing at any moment. The air was fairly pure, but I could see no sign of animal life. The boom of the water, bouncing back off these innumerable rocky facets, filled the grotto with weird echoes, under which ran a steady murmuring ground-bass.

I would not risk a descent into the pool, since I was by no means sure whether I could get up again unaided. I did, however, manage to lean far enough over the edge to explore part of the bottom with my pole. There was not a grain of sand there; what I found was a hard, granitelike surface about a yard below the surface of the water.

I committed the grotto's dimensions and topography to memory, and then began the return journey—this time an ascent on my stomach. They must have been getting worried about me on top; they conveyed as much by jerking hard at the rope. Getting up was easier and quicker than coming down. When at last I stumbled out into daylight I flung myself at my companions and embraced them from sheer relief.

The next day Antu and I made the descent together. We tied the bucket and shovel to the end of another rope, and also linked ourselves together for greater security, like mountaineers. We had with us the shovel handle and a crowbar. Antu was scared, but this time I felt calm enough myself to reassure him. When we reached the edge of the pool we lashed the rope around a projecting horn of rock and swung ourselves down. The water was icy cold, and reached our waists.

While Antu banged away at one spot with the crowbar, I concluded my investigation of the bottom. It formed a single hard, compact, diamond-bearing formation from side to side. We filled the bucket and signaled to Lolomai to haul it up. She sent it back stacked with palm leaves: evidently it had reached the surface half empty, and she meant us to cover the contents with the leaves to prevent spilling.

We sent up five bucketfuls, one after the other; but we could not stick it any longer after that, on account of the cold. As soon as we were back on top we began the washing. From this scanty sample we collected three two-carat diamonds and about ten small gold nuggets in the middle sieve, while the bottom one yielded a score of small diamonds and a sizable quantity of gold dust. It was not hard to imagine the amount we could hope to find if we continued our prospecting from such a source. Anyone who succeeded in clearing that pool singlehanded would find more gold and diamonds there than he could amass in a lifetime's work anywhere else.

Those were wonderful days. Antu and I took turns down in the pool, staying there just long enough to send up four or five bucketfuls of shale. Our stock of gold and diamonds rose visibly. Food presented no problem: game was plentiful, the river swarmed with fish, and the forest supplied all the fresh fruit we needed. The snakes, which prefer a quiet life, had removed themselves from our sphere of operations, the big cats made their presence felt only at night, and I was now sufficiently accustomed to mosquitoes to put up with them at a pinch. My present was fully occupied and my life my own; a future such as I had never dreamed of lay before me, haloed with the fabulous aura that surrounds diamonds.

While I wove fantasies of wealth to come, I could imagine nothing better for the present than long afternoons with Lolomai in our private Eden, watching the jungle animals come down to disport themselves by the river. I had learned to recognize a good proportion of these regular visitors, and some of them had become quite familiar friends. I would see them peep timidly out from the paths that led across the small jungle glades behind the foreshore: they would peer cautiously around for a moment, then finally trot down to drink at the water's edge. There was a female porcupine that had all the natural instincts of a high-class tart; she would come down one of the tracks looking like a small prickly ball, and when she reached the point where her track crossed another one she would stop and peer anxiously in both directions. The moment she spotted her boy-friend approaching she would hurry off to meet him in a state of pure ecstasy. By a series of coquettish leaps and bounds she did her best to draw him toward the intersection point of the two tracks, and there—still tempting him on, but retreating whenever he got too close—she paused from time to time, turning her head in the direction of the other track. In vain did the male porcupine try to lure her down to the stream. His lady-love would neither abandon her own campaign nor allow him to get away when he showed signs of impatience. She would frisk around him for a moment, then flounce off, looking back over one shoulder, in an effort to lead him toward her own favorite spot. She went on like this till another male porcupine appeared on the scene, at which point she would instantly leave the first one in the lurch and make up to the new arrival, conquering him within a matter of moments by precisely the same methods. The deserted male would sit up on his hind legs and wave his front paws in the air as though appealing to her, over and over again, rubbing his snout, waving his tail, and from time to time scraping the ground as though to sharpen up his claws. There he remained, not budging an inch, ready to take on the pair of them. But no sooner had the female switched her favors to the second porcupine than—presto!—she dropped him again and returned to the first one, as though begging forgiveness for her little escapade. More coaxing tricks, and then back to Number Two; and so on, to and fro, till both males flew at each other in a fury, quills erect. When battle was joined the female stood to one side and watched the contest like a rather absent-minded referee. It was not a battle to the death; one of the two, after a more or less severe mauling, would surrender the field, whereupon the little trollop, more full of airs and graces than ever, would finally prink off down to the stream with the victor.

The birds were always there to give the alarm in an emergency, and this produced a general stampede. The only animals that stayed put were the porcupines, quills bristling at every point, and the armadillos, which rolled themselves into a defensive ball of armor. If no danger threatened, on the other hand, they would all disport themselves on the beach till dusk, and then it was the appearance of the bats that heralded their departure.

One evening they all had gone except for one flying squirrel, who had his dray in a hollow tree nearby. He was busily nibbling at what looked like a carob, while his mate looked down on him from the nest, chattering uneasily. Suddenly the mournful call of a screech owl made him look up, and he saw a pair of these terrible night hunters staring straight at him, their eyes gleaming like two sets of headlamps. He took a leap in the direction of his dray, just as the first owl spread its wings and launched itself in pursuit. But a split second before its talons could close on the little animal, the other squirrel plummeted down from the tree, landing fair and square on its back. They rolled over on the ground in a flurry of fur and feathers, and the squirrel might well have escaped had the owl's companion not joined in the fray; with one terrible dart of its beak it tore the small rodent to shreds.

The whole episode happened so quickly that I had no time to intervene. In any case, I knew very well that such intervention would have been futile. This was the law of the jungle, and no creature that dwelt in the forest could escape it.

We had been encamped below Diamond Mountain for about four months. The animals' mating season was long since over, and now their young began to appear on the scene. There was a big wildcat that was always prowling around this area, and the newborn, inexperienced cubs gave him some easy hunting. He was dark gray in color, with black spots, a splendid head, pointed ears, and a fine set of whiskers, while his tail flicked constantly from side to side, like a restless snake. I had been waiting to get a shot at him for some time: I wanted to stop his marauding activities against the smaller riverbank fauna. One day I was out hunting with Antu, not far from the sandy spit, when we suddenly spotted the wildcat through a gap in the undergrowth, about twenty yards away. He was lying stretched out sunning himself on a tree trunk that had blown down in the winter gales. Antu raised his bow and took aim, but at that moment the cat got up, stretched itself, yawned, licked around its chops and shoulders, and was just on the point of settling down again when it heard a faint crackle of twigs. It pricked up its ears and prowled off. The sound came steadily nearer. With one bound the wildcat sprang up into a handy tree, where it crouched motionless, so well camouflaged that after a while we were unable to detect it. In a moment the bushes parted and there emerged a small doe, followed by two fawns, which wandered uneasily around for a moment and then came prinking back to their mother again. The cat watched them, itself as motionless as a statue. But the moment the little group passed under the tree it sprang, and a split second later its sharp teeth had sunk in the neck of the fawn that was lagging a little behind the other two. The doe turned back to the rescue, but the wildcat was by now back up the tree again, the little fawn gripped tight in its talons. It was at this moment that Antu's arrow whistled through the air, piercing the wildcat's skull from side to side. The cat fell to earth without uttering a sound, its prey still held in its claws. The doe sprang back, alarmed, but at once returned to where its fawn lay. It nuzzled the little creature all over, several times, and with loving tenderness tried to shake it into consciousness; but alas, the fawn was already dead.

I was so fully immersed in the life of the forest that I felt I had lived there all my life and would remain there forever. I felt strong and healthy, and was bursting with a vigor I had never before possessed. My regular bouts with the insatiable Lolomai left me plenty of spare energy for the relatively little work that remained indispensable. Close contact with nature induced a mood of absolute happiness and satisfaction in me. By knowing God's creatures I felt I had come nearer to God, and my heart was at peace. And though I made no formal prayers, I gave God silent thanks for my good fortune, several times a day.

We continued to prospect down in the pool. By now constant familiarity with it had altogether dispelled our fear, and as a result we stepped up the pace of our work: every day we now hauled up at least ten bucketfuls of shale for washing. But however hard we labored there was no chance of our getting down to the lowest strata of the formation before the rainy season—and it was there, beyond any doubt, that the really big diamonds lay hidden.

Lometai was a model wife: she learned all she could from me that might help her to make Antu's life more pleasant and comfortable. When Lolomai and I were making love, I noticed that she would hide in the bushes and spy on us. Lolomai must have told her something in confidence that aroused her womanly curiosity—and envy. Lolomai herself gave me deeper satisfaction every time we slept together, and I could never have enough of her. There was a rare harmony between us at the emotional no less than at the physical level: our desire was in tune with our affections, and both with the world of nature around us. Lolomai's instinctive attitude to life and unspoiled simpleheartedness remained quite astounding. The only factor complicating them was the sense of modesty she had learned from me, and this merely served to increase my affection for her. In any case our relationship did not involve any hint of feminine "submission." For the first time in my life, by a curious combination of circumstances, I felt I was living, not for any extraneous purpose or future prospect, but with the spontaneous felicity of a waterfall or tree. And—unlike the tree—I was aware of my good fortune, and rejoiced in it.

One day Antu and I were down by the river, sifting the shale we had collected earlier that morning. Our attention was suddenly distracted from our work by a confused yowling noise, which I thought might indicate the presence of another wildcat. But Antu pointed to a group of young alligators, frolicking about in a stretch of water that was overhung by a fallen tree, another storm casualty. Just at this moment Lolomai and Lometai came up. Like all the natives of this area, they regarded cayman's tail as a great delicacy, and begged Antu to catch one for them. While Antu was preparing a kind of lasso from liana rope, Lolomai walked out along the trunk, balancing with her arms, till she reached the point where the branches and foliage began, almost exactly over the gamboling alligators.

For no good reason I suddenly felt scared, and shouted to Lolomai to come back. She smiled at me reassuringly and even started to do comic balancing tricks. His lasso now ready, Antu sprang onto the trunk himself, while Lolomai stood there holding on by the foliage. They were over a yard above the surface of the water, and it was not very difficult to slip the lasso over one of the young caymans, which they then proceeded to haul up, wriggling and thrashing like a mad thing.

At that moment the mother alligator appeared. In her efforts to rescue her offspring she reared right up out of the water, till her jaws almost touched Antu. The Indian quickly made his way back to the foot of the trunk, but the alligator, far from desisting, now proceeded to vent her wrath on Lolomai. Luckily, she was incapable of getting up onto the trunk itself: every time she tried she flopped back heavily into the water. Lolomai finally realized that she might be wise to retreat. I followed her movements with agonized apprehension; I could not at first screw myself up to leave her and go back for my rifle. At last I tore myself away, and an instant later heard a shriek of horror: with its highest jump so far the alligator had severely shaken the tree trunk, just as Lolomai was on the part that Antu had traversed a moment or so before. His wet feet had left it dangerously slippery. I was just in time to see Lolomai falling, and the alligator waiting for her with open jaws. They both vanished together in a swirl of muddy water. Antu, who was nearer than I was, dropped the baby cayman and plunged after them, brandishing his knife.

Meanwhile the howls of the frantic alligator had brought others to the scene. I trained my rifle on them and emptied the magazine: five shots, and I had no more ammunition, since my cartridge belts were back at the hut. Still, at least there was now no danger from stray alligators. I dived into the river just as Antu was coming up for breath. It was impossible to see a thing under water, but I swam down and stabbed frantically with my knife at something clinging to the bottom which might have been the body of the mother alligator. Then I came up to the surface for air, and Antu went down again. Lometai was on the bank, pointing: she had seen something being whirled downstream by the fast current. I swam and swam, with every ounce of strength I possessed. About fifty yards lower down I caught up with Lolomai's body, and managed to drag it ashore. She gave not the slightest sign of life. Her chest was ripped open and drenched with blood. I stanched her wounds as best I could and then, idiotically, began to try artificial respiration on her.

The dog had jumped in the river when we did. That was the last we ever saw of it.

I looked, but would not see: I refused to credit the evidence of my senses. There before me lay my little Lolomai, stiff and lifeless, whose voice had once been light as the wind that rustled through the leaves of the forest. Lolomai always embodied at least two opposites, being at once thoughtless and vigilant, blending fear with serenity. Sometimes she would, quite unexpectedly, flit off a jungle track into the undergrowth, a lithe shadow, her body not so much as brushing the tangled stems that swallowed her up.

With her death my ties with the forest were broken, the sense of belonging destroyed. Now I should return among the Taurepán as a stranger, a white man in search of diamonds, wealth beyond the range of their comprehension. We buried her beneath the great tree in whose shade we had so often lain, wrapped in the grass mat that she had woven with her own hands. All the time a deep fear was growing within me, a fear of diamonds and the curse they seemed to carry with them. Kaicusé had died on the morning that we found a large stone; just before Lolomai's death we had come upon another. Antu said this was the work of Canaima.

On the fourth day after Lolomai's burial, I could not stand it any longer and called to Antu at dawn:

"Let us leave."

"Yes, let us leave," he answered promptly, "we cannot stay here any longer."

Right after breakfast we began to strike camp. Our bucket and shovel were still in the shaft, which we had not revisited since Lolomai's death. Now we had to retrieve them. As I climbed down somewhat reluctantly, I was amazed to find, not far from the entrance, that the narrow passage was blocked

by a big rock. I tried all around it with my bare feet. There was
no space left. I climbed up again to tell Antu, who wanted to
see for himself but soon came back with the same news.

I wanted to be quite sure in view of the future and went
down a second time to explore the situation. I could not go
head foremost and make use of my hands, because the sheer
drop made it impossible to come back again that way. Nor
could I take a torch, since its fumes would have made me suf-
focate. I tried again to explore from all sides with my feet.
There seemed not the smallest crevice left. I tried to push the
rock, but it did not budge an inch. The entrance to the precious
pool was solidly blocked. If nothing had happened to Lolomai,
it was quite probable that Antu and I would have been down
in the grotto when the fall occurred, and we should have remained there forever.

Chapter 10

♦

ANTU IN CARACAS

Our journey back was silent and uneventful.

I knew something had happened the moment we reached the outskirts of the village, and I saw the women wearing—or, to be more accurate, swathed in—some sort of red cotton stuff from the waist downward. In the middle of the crowd that had gathered on the riverbank to welcome us there stood a white man, with the tall, hard, gaunt sort of figure that somewhat resembles an iron rivet. He had reddish hair and a large, sharp nose. While we were disembarking Mundo and the witch doctor appeared, both of them wearing shirts and pants.

For a moment I supposed that the white man was a diamond prospector like myself, and the idea did not appeal to me. When Mundo, having greeted me, turned aside to speak to Antu and Lometai, this person came over and began to address me in English.

"Pleased to meet you," he said. "My name's John Burlay. I'm an Evangelical missionary. Been here about three weeks. Came across from British Guiana. What's your religion?"

"I'm a Catholic," I told him.

"Fine, fine," he declared. "The Word of Christ must be spread throughout the world. I am relying on your help to bring the Gospel to these poor savages."

"Plenty of time," I said.

But he was off again, muttering something about eternal damnation. Feeling decidedly irritated, I cut into this harangue, saying we must talk about the matter some other time.

Mundo presented a most dandified appearance. I couldn't understand it. I took him off to my hut, and there told him the story of our tragic trip. But he was so preoccupied that he paid scant attention to my news, and even Lolomai's death made practically no impression on him. Indeed, hardly had I concluded my tale when—without so much as a by-your-leave—he launched into his own. The missionary had arrived three weeks earlier, escorted by four Europeanized Indians of the same ethnic group as the Taurepán, who understood their language. His first act had been to distribute clothes all around. That evening he had the whole tribe assembled, and one of his acolytes told them stories from the life of Christ and gave them some instruction in psalm singing. I was far too intrigued by this story to realize that Mundo was keeping something back.

That evening John Burlay paid me a visit in my hut, and described his journey—over Roraima, the nine-thousand-foot peak between British Guiana, Brazil, and the Venezuelan Gran Sabana, and thence through the forest to the Uai-parú. I listened to his tale, though my main concern was to judge his sincerity from his tone of voice. Presently the time for his prayer meeting arrived, and he invited me to join him.

His assistants had assembled the tribe before an altar on which there stood a large crucifix. All the natives listened with the most raptly devoted air of piety imaginable, and at the end we all, myself included, cried "Hallelujah!"

In those three weeks John Burlay had revolutionized a tribal society that had previously remained static for centuries. No one now made love in public, as they used to do. The men did not even bathe with the women down at the river. In a few days, and without any trouble, he had managed to abolish polygamy and baptize the whole lot of them. If I had stayed much longer his evangelical fervor would have converted me, as well. He pursued his task with the methodical indifference of a dedicated man (his faith was the sort that moves mountains), and the Taurepán responded as willingly as children who have been given a nice present, and are then offered a complete change of life. All this by itself was enough to put me out of sorts; and I had other suspicions about him, too.

As soon as I could I slipped away from the prayer meeting and went for a stroll through the village. My self-esteem received a certain fillip from what I saw. It was not only the missionary who had changed this people's ways; they had followed my advice as well. I found large enclosures filled with wild boar, *lapa, chigüire,* and vast numbers of woodcock. I was contemplating this lot when a woman called out to me: would I go and take a look at her son, who was very ill? I followed her into the hut, and found a young man with a leaf plaster on his shoulder. When I stripped it off I stood rooted to the ground with sheer astonishment: what he was suffering from was, undoubtedly, a gunshot wound.

Gangrene had set in, and there was nothing I could do for him. But I was even more concerned by the nature of his complaint. The only gun around the place was my rifle, and I had had it with me the whole time. Then I thought of the missionary and his assistants. As soon as the service was over I questioned them.

"We go through the world bearing the Cross of Christ," I was told. "We do not carry guns." And that was that.

It was only then that I remembered Mundo's extraordinary getup: he had been wearing mosquito boots and a sombrero. I asked the missionary whether he had given them to him.

"No. The only presents we have given out are machetes, a knife or two, and some mirrors and red cloth for the women."

Then he went back with me to the hut where the boy lay, and came to the same conclusion as I had done: the wound had undoubtedly been caused by a bullet, and there was nothing that could be done at this stage to save the victim.

I left Burlay to his prayers and hurried off to find Mundo.

"Who shot that boy?" I asked him, without any preliminaries.

He tried to mutter some sort of excuse at first; then, when he saw how furious I was, he realized that his lies would not pass muster, and decided to make a clean breast of the whole affair. They had gone out hunting, a few hours' march beyond the river, and suddenly found themselves face to face with a couple of half-breeds, guns at the ready. When Mundo and his men told them to drop their weapons, they had opened fire. A regular battle followed, during which both the half-breeds were killed. Losses on Mundo's side were one man killed, and one wounded—the latter being the boy I had recently visited.

"Let's get this straight," I said. "Those pants and boots and hat you're wearing—did they belong to those half-breeds?"

"Yes."

"What else did you get off them?"

Reluctantly Mundo stooped down and rolled back the mat, revealing two carbines (without any ammunition), two sieves, in excellent condition, a *batea* for sifting gold dust, two shovels, a pick, and a crowbar. The carbines were of Brazilian manufacture. Finally Mundo brought out a small pot that contained about fifteen carats of diamonds.

I realized it was no use taking a high moral line with him: I might as well save my breath. He would not understand a word I said, and in any case it was the missionary's business to look after these people's souls. So I limited myself to asking him what he had done with the bodies. Next day, accompanied by the missionary and one of the Indians who had taken part in the skirmish, we went out into the forest to bury the dead men and see if they had any documents on them by which they might be identified. But all we found were their clean-picked bones.

By way of retribution we had to listen to a long sermon that evening in the village on the punishments that God and man reserve for those who kill their fellows.

When I was back in my own hut a very simple thought struck me. I had arrived from the north, and the missionary from the east. The two dead prospectors came up from the south, probably across the Sierra Pacaraima. Westward, toward the Orinoco, the obstacles were probably no more insurmountable. It was clear that Taurepán could in fact be reached from every quarter of the compass. The Brazilians had been unlucky, but others would follow in their tracks; and once the word got around that diamonds were to be found here, adventurers of every race and color would soon be descending on the area. Even the missionary, with all his sanctimonious airs, now struck me as highly suspect. No doubt about it, he and his crew were altogether too inquisitive.

I had not much time left in which to act. I made up my mind that same evening to return to Caracas. I would tell no one of my plans except Antu: I had promised that I would take him with me, to the "land of blonde women, with blue eyes and white breasts." When I spoke of such things he was all enthusiasm. We would build a light canoe, two of his fellow tribesmen would carry it on their shoulders as far as the Hacha, and from thence forward we would be on our own.

When the boat was ready I explained to Mundo the motives that compelled my departure, and also tried to make him understand what a fine experience it would be for Antu to spend some time in a big city, where he would learn endless useful lessons that could later be imparted to his fellow tribesmen. Then I took him with me to a yuca-field not far from the village. Here there was a stretch of uneven ground about six hundred yards long—quite sufficient, once it had been leveled out, to make an airstrip. I explained what an airplane was, and showed him the way to strip off the undergrowth and brushwood, and level the ground. If he did the work thoroughly, I told him, he would presently see me return from the air, and then an era of prosperity and well-being would begin for him and all his people.

He was not the same suspicious character who had greeted me on my first arrival, impassive of feature and fanatically hostile to all Europeans. Perhaps he was getting older; perhaps all these deaths around him, and the innovations the tribe was undergoing, had between them undermined his self-confidence. He promised me he would do all he could to get the airstrip ready, and he was only too glad for Antu to come with me. By now the entire village knew of our imminent departure.

The following morning everyone turned up on the village square to say good-by to us. Urulai wept as she embraced me. I felt moved myself by this leavetaking, and tears sprang to my eyes also, melting the hard lump I had carried in my throat for the last few weeks. Only she and Antu had really shared my grief at the death of Lolomai; and I cherished a genuine feeling of affection for her, too. During this period, after my return, she had been extremely thoughtful on my behalf, always there beside me, but invariably conveying the impression of not wanting to renew or trespass on my memories of Lolomai.

Though I did not find the same primitive, warmhearted, happy-go-lucky atmosphere as I once had done, I nevertheless realized how intimate were the links that bound me to these people, and how much the period I had spent among them meant to me. Now I was a European again, a white man, a *racional* whose prime concern was the best way of despoiling the area of its riches. But I was by no means so sure that the fulfillment of my plans would prove an advantage for the Taurepán themselves. Certainly I had helped them more by teaching them to make brooms and domesticate animals.

Our tiny caravan set off toward the north, and very soon the dense green jungle swallowed us up. The little village of the Taurepán lay beyond the river, and we were alone in the forest once more.

Ten days later, with the canoe leaking at every joint, we reached Francisco's village. Francisco himself no longer recognized me. When he realized who I was, he went into transports of delight and amazement that would have been more fitting had I risen from the dead. Then he hurried off to fetch José, Antonio, and Angelito, who couldn't believe that I had really showed up again. When they left me at the Hacha River they were quite convinced I would never reach my goal, and had long since assumed that I was dead. They were the first people who told me how much I had changed: I had become a great deal thinner, and was so tanned by sun and wind that I could have passed as a half-breed.

In Francisco's village Antu got his first glimpses of civilization: hens, sows, rice, pasta, all of them things he had never seen before in his life.

Our trip had been far from uneventful. The current spun our canoe down through the rapids, and on four separate occasions we had capsized, despite Antu's great skill and his timely avoidance of whirlpools. One morning we had been carried into a wall of rock, and were obliged to make extensive repairs to the entire canoe. Twice we had been attacked by jaguars, and one morning we woke up to find ourselves surrounded by alligators. I had kept my original promise and left Mundo my rifle, but he had let me keep the Brazilians' carbines.

So, through God's grace, we finally reached Francisco's village, with my pouches of gold and diamonds securely fastened, one of them to Antu's belt and the other to my own.

Late that afternoon we pushed on to Uriman, where we sold a few ounces of gold, bought ourselves some new clothes, and had a high old time during the evening. Antu was desperately anxious to pick up the least particle of information that might benefit his people, and probably saw the proceedings through rose-tinted spectacles.

Next morning the local miners and prospectors came around and questioned me closely. Some of them recalled having seen me the previous year with Cardona, and they exuded curiosity and suspicion from every pore. Despite my evasive replies, I had no doubt that many of them would at once set off into the unknown. It was clear that very little would suffice to stir them into action: the merest hint was enough, let alone a full-blown rumor of El Dorado.

Two days later a Dakota belonging to Linea Aeropostale Venezuelana arrived, and Antu's eyes bulged in amazement as he watched "the big bird that roars" touch down. Two hours later we were landing at Ciudad Bolívar. Poor Antu, hampered by his unfamiliar shoes and clothes, carried himself as stiffly as a tailor's dummy, and looked, I fear, faintly ridiculous. Every few moments he would stop and stand stock-still, eying the traffic, the cars, the shop windows, the people hurrying by. While we were in Ciudad Bolívar I reported my finds to the appropriate official department. This was the first step toward obtaining the concession for the area. Two days later we were in Caracas.

The city had changed vastly even in a year, taking further giant strides toward becoming a major modern metropolis. I took Antu everywhere with me, and for the first few days he seemed content to look and learn. Then he began to acquire a bewildered look, and was no longer capable of getting his bearings among all these new sights: he seemed exhausted rather than inquisitive. Here no one took any special notice of him; he was one among many, lost in the crowd. But he always stayed close beside me, and if I left him on his own in the house, very soon he would come looking for me in my favorite bar, where he could be sure of finding me with my friends. He was a fish out of water here. In the forest he feared nothing; here the mere idea of crossing a street or boarding a bus terrified him. My Caracas friends to whom I had introduced him regarded him as a figure of fun; Antu knew this, and was hurt by it, and I suffered too, because of his distress.

Though he was a handsome, well-knit youth, none of the fabulous blonde women he had dreamed about vouchsafed him so much as a glance. I realized that he was daily becoming more depressed, that his nerves could not stand the tainted air, the endless clamor and confusion. I blamed myself for ever having brought him with me, but I never summoned up enough courage to discuss the matter with him.

Then one morning he came and woke me up and said: "I want to go back to my own people." He had learned a great deal during the month he had spent in Caracas, he told me, but now he had had enough of it. He wanted to leave right away—though he was determined to take everything he could carry with him.

He had a plane all to himself for the flight between Caracas and Uriman. There he would contact Francisco, and with three or four canoes and an escort would transport all his newly acquired possessions as far as he could by water. After that he would go on ahead and bring back some of his own people, and they would hump his gear the rest of the way to Taurepán. Before he went aboard the plane I embraced him.

I obtained concessions for five claims from the government, each claim being of 999 acres and situated on the Brazilian frontier, between the Rio Blanco and the Uai-parú. Thus I found myself the owner of a large territory that I knew to be rich in gold and diamonds. I had become a man without financial worries.

Chapter 11

♦

RETURN TO THE UAI-PARÚ

I had been in Caracas for about a year when I walked into the Don Luis Bar one evening and found Vaughan there. The papers had printed stories about my exploits, and the American was furious.

"Journalist, eh?" he said. "More fool me, believing my friends."

"Still doing trips in that old rattletrap?" I asked him.

He went bright purple. "My plane," he said, "will go on flying while it still has a drop of gas in its works. A single drop, d'you understand?"

Poor Vaughan: he simply couldn't bear hearing anybody make fun of his plane. When he had calmed down a bit and was capable of taking in what I said, I asked whether he would co-operate with me on a return trip to the Uai-parú.

To begin with, I cut him in on the profits of the concessions. Then together we arranged to take along a geologist (known as Pop), and two surveyors, an Italian called Tommasino, and Mayer, who was German. The latter had agreed to fix the boundaries of the concession for me. We agreed that the three of them were to wait at Uriman while we pushed on to the Taurepán village and examined the state of the trail.

Having made our arrangements, we took off a few days later. The aircraft exceeded all our expectations. After a rather shaky start we went roaring away along the course of the Caroní River, while the surveyors waved to us from the overgrown track that led to Uriman. Vaughan, who appeared to be more relaxed now I had become easier myself, began to chatter with cheerful loquacity. He had fought in Italy, he told me, and had had his uniform pinched in Naples, but it wasn't really fair to take it out on me for that, was it? It wasn't my fault. The only thing I could think about while he was talking was the airstrip we would have to come down on. I had given Antu numerous detailed instructions about this during our stay in Caracas, but I was by no means sure how many of them he would manage to carry out. If it proved impossible to use the strip, we would have to turn back, and the interminable green jungle stretching out beneath us was not exactly the best place for a forced landing.

Now we had Mt. Auyán-Tepuy ahead of us, a dizzily high peak, from the summit of which a cascade of gleaming white water fell over two thousand feet in a cloud of foam and spray, iridescent at dawn with all the colors of the rainbow. This was the famous Angel Falls, named after the American pilot, Jimmy Angel, who had first landed there. As reckless a man as Vaughan, but more disposed than Vaughan was to place credence in local legends, Angel had picked up some tale in the Gran Sabana about the summit of the mountain being littered with gold nuggets, and made up his mind to fly there with a copilot and see for himself. Their aircraft was wrecked on landing, and the two fliers were rescued, some days later, by Cardona, who happened to be in the area and had organized a search party.

"I'll show you Jimmy's plane," Vaughan yelled above the roar of the engine.

"Don't bother," I said, hastily. "It doesn't matter."

But he insisted on diving down to within a few yards of the summit of the narrow plateau, so that we could see the remains of the aircraft still lying there. It seemed to me mere pointless exhibitionism to perform such aerobatics in an old rattletrap like the one Vaughan flew; and the air of wry and pitying contempt with which the American viewed my obvious alarm I found intensely irritating.

Vaughan went on and on like a dripping tap: he seemed

unable to stop talking. Now his theme was Italian signorinas and their amatory prowess: still, irksome though his monologizing was, at least it distracted him from doing any more show-off stunts. Then, suddenly, we found ourselves passing through a cloud, and unable to see farther than the nose of the plane. Squalls of heavy driving rain beat down all around us, to a continual accompaniment of thunder and lightning. The sky seemed one gigantic colander, and we got soaked to the skin. Even Vaughan now abandoned his pose of gay relaxation, and sat hunched over the controls.

As abruptly as it had begun, the storm ended, and we found ourselves out in bright sunshine once more. Below us we could see the junction of the Icaparú and Caroní Rivers. We set our course by this landmark and flew on at low level, through whole squadrons of parrots, which scattered in terror at our approach. I kept a sharp lookout now, since we could not be far from the Hacha, where we were due to turn south till we struck the Rio Blanco. I found it easy to recognize the country below me: after my first trip I remembered every yard of the route.

We flew over the mountain range, sped across the Rio Blanco and a stretch of forest beyond it, till there, at last, were the cluster of hut roofs that marked the site of my village. Vaughan came in directly over the huts, and at the sound of the aircraft everyone rushed out, waving frantically. But when we actually touched down the natives fled, panic-stricken, and only Antu remained out there to welcome us.

The strip had been prepared as I ordered. Vaughan made four low-level runs to inspect it. Then he came in to land. *"Buena suerte!"* I muttered, shifting myself into the least dangerous position possible. He was going to need some luck, at that. I watched with bated breath as he positioned himself for the run-in, and commended my soul to God. But Vaughan knew his job all right. He skimmed in just above the treetops, touched ground, bounced, settled down, and went bumping along the strip. The plane lost speed and with a great squealing of brakes came to a halt about two feet short of an enormous tree. We had made it.

All the Taurepán now came running out toward the plane. I unbuckled my safety belt, jumped down, and found myself in Antu's arms. The rest of them halted some twenty yards away from the plane—all except Mundo, who advanced in his usual taciturn fashion, but gave me an effusive welcome nevertheless. Then Urulai detached herself from the crowd, and very timidly, eyes modestly lowered, came forward and knelt at my feet. She had waited for me all this time. I was back home again.

Two winters had passed since my departure, but things remained very much as I had left them. People had got married, and a few new huts had been erected as a result. One or two women who did not speak Taurepán—imports from some tribe beyond the frontier—were now going about the village, gradually getting themselves acclimatized to their new surroundings. The carbines and ammunition were now quite useless. The hens and ducks and turkeys that Antu brought back with him had been eaten by pumas and ocelots. Everything was as it had formerly been, and the tribe had cheerfully reverted to its old ways. There was no surviving trace of the missionary and his activities. The hut with the crucifix and altar had been destroyed, and the natives had turned back to Mauri and Canaima, who clearly satisfied their religious aspirations. The women bathed with the men again, and everyone cheerfully copulated in public.

Perhaps because he was very much wrapped up in a new, extremely youthful wife, Mundo had gone into semi-retirement, leaving a good proportion of his chiefly duties to Antu, who now—as far as his fellow tribesmen were concerned—symbolized the world of civilization and progress.

On my first expedition the long and exhausting trek through the forest had prepared me, both physically and psychologically, for a primitive way of life. This time, however, I was fresh from the easy life of a big city and comfortable hotels; and the process of adaptation (or so I feared) was liable to require more time and effort.

Vaughan's plane had bogged down in the soft earth of the

airstrip. For three days men, women, and children toiled frantically to get it clear and to put the strip itself in proper order once more. They even abandoned the yuca harvest, which was their normal occupation at this time of year. The American showed them how to enlarge the runway, and made them strengthen its surface with layers of river gravel, which they then rolled flat, using large tree trunks in lieu of rollers. Finally he took off without trouble. He would be back in a week's time with Pop, and on subsequent trips he was to ferry in the two surveyors.

I was excited by the idea of using this airstrip to bring the blessings and benefits of civilization to the Indians: clothes, for instance, and medical assistance, especially for the children. God knows they needed such things. I felt it would be a real achievement to bring them out of their isolation and make them an integral part of the country to which, after all, they belonged. I discussed these schemes with Antu, who very soon became as enthusiastic about them as I was. Even the witch doctor, who was an intelligent man, regarded me as a friend and gave me his wholehearted co-operation. It was Mundo who eventually threw cold water on my ideas.

He came around to my hut one day and told me what frightened him about such a prospect. He did not care for the idea of living in constant contact with a stream of white visitors, all drawn by the alluring mirage of diamonds: he was afraid that his people would suffer from such an influx. From my own point of view, on the other hand, I could not possibly do without European technical aid. I wanted to make probes in certain forest valleys that had, beyond a shadow of doubt, once formed the beds of long-vanished rivers. Fairly large holes must be drilled through the outer crust before one could get to the formation proper, which sometimes lay as much as ten or twelve yards beneath the surface; then an estimate had to be made, from samples, of the amount of diamonds it contained; and finally, if the test showed it was worth it, the crust had to be broken up and removed. There was also the business of exploring the very deep pools to be found on the existing river bed; that was a technical job, too.

The natives were not accustomed to sustained work, and in any case would be of very little use to me. Finally I hit on what seemed to me a fair solution of the problem. I would build a camp for white visitors, about half a mile away, out of sight across the river, and forbid them all access to the native village.

Mundo seemed satisfied with this decision, though privately I was by no means sure that I would be able to maintain a barrier between the two communities. But I had no alternative, and so I set to work at once. There was far too much at stake for me to be deterred merely by scruples on behalf of a few Indians. In any case, I was convinced that they would learn a great deal from the experiment, and all to their own advantage.

Chapter 12

◆

THE MINING CAMP

Vaughan arrived punctually at the end of the week, bringing not only the geologist but also a small supply of provisions and some axes. He gave the airstrip full marks this time, and reported that several mining experts had asked if he would fly them out to the concession. He took off again almost at once, and returned next day with Tommasino and a bundle of saws. Three days later he flew in the second surveyor, Mayer.

During the two days he stayed between flights he helped us to get the camp ready. We stripped the area of trees and brushwood, and burned it off to drive away snakes. Then we built one big wooden hut in the middle, to serve as a store-room and kitchen, another for the geologist (who would also be in charge of the camp), and a third for the two surveyors. Around these we erected several others, each with accommodation for about ten people.

We laid on a supply of fresh water from a stream up the hillside, piping it down to the camp with a series of jointed bamboos. Vaughan, meanwhile, had decided to purchase a twin-engined Canadian plane that had a much greater load-capacity than his ancient crate, and this meant lengthening the runway. Having smelled money in the air, he was anxious to fly in as much gear and labor as he could, and without delay.

I continued to live in the village, with Urulai. I went out in the morning to work on the campsite, and came back in the evening. The other three Europeans had already settled down in their huts, and were cooking for themselves. Sometimes they invited Mundo or Antu along, and stuffed them with *spaghetti al sugo* and large helpings of meat or fish. All the natives were glutted with our provisions, which we doled out to them in return for their labor. We mixed up flour and water and a little fat and fried the result: this was our bread. But we hardly ever managed to eat any, since the Indians would watch us cooking it, wide-eyed, and we had to share it out among them. Most times they somehow got the lot. They had the habits of small children and the inquisitiveness of monkeys: they wanted to try anything new that came their way. They were not outstanding workers, since work was a habit they had never acquired; but they were certainly willing, and the project went ahead with surprising speed. We built a poultry yard, fencing it in really strongly so that wild beasts could not raid it as they had done with the pens put up by the Indians. We also planned to strip another stretch of forest and turn it into a large kitchen garden.

On one of his trips Vaughan brought along a rather unusual type of adventurer, a former banker from Turin, who had gone badly bankrupt and had now settled in eastern Venezuela, where he made a living as a *pulpero,* or general grocer. He had the banker's robust good sense coupled with the affable nature one so often finds among citizens of Turin; he offered to set up a general store in the camp, stock it with goods, and conduct a private retail trade for the benefit of the mining community.

Since it was clear that I would never have time to deal with the provisioning myself, I was quite glad to grant him the concession, in return for a percentage of his turnover. Later I discovered that it was he who had put up the capital for Vaughan to purchase the Canadian plane. Another one who had his nose to the ground and smelled cash. With the arrival of a trader the seeds of civilization—our civilization, of course —had truly been sown; and this, in a quiet way, was to be the point from which corruption spread.

Finally, after forty days' hard work, camp and airstrip were ready. The two surveyors now set out, with their measuring instruments and carbines, to mark out the boundaries of the concession. I sent along two young Indians with them, who had already got used to white men's ways through working with us, and who would assist them to dig trenches and blaze trees as boundary marks. They took a week's provisions with them. At seven-day intervals they would come down the valley as far as the river, where a canoe would meet them with further supplies of fresh food, and bring back news of their health and progress.

For some little while now there had been no sign of Vaughan. I realized he must have gone north to Canada to pick up the new plane; but I awaited his return with impatience, since I had entrusted him with the job of finding a doctor prepared to take up residence on the Uai-parú. I wanted to make some immediate reparation to the Taurepán for having introduced modern commerce among them.

One morning we heard a roar of engines in the sky, somewhat louder than usual, and a moment later there was the brand-new aircraft on the strip. When Vaughan got out he was accompanied not only by the banker-turned-storekeeper, but also by a bespectacled young Spaniard called Beato, who turned out to be the doctor. A large hut had been set aside for his infirmary and living quarters, and he moved in at once, while Vaughan and the storekeeper were unloading cases and sacks from the plane and humping them across to the *pulperia*.

We were all set.

Throughout this period of hard work I had had little time to devote to Urulai. When I got home in the evening I was tired out, and only wanted to get to bed and sleep. Just occasionally, in the brief period after supper before sleep claimed me, I found myself wondering why—despite everything—it was all so different from the old days. When had that idyllic existence come to an end? I turned sentimental, evoking memories of Lolomai, brooding with pleasurable nostalgia over the past. One evening, at this point in my reverie, an undertone of sadness crept in: I no longer felt so sure that I was acting for the good of the Taurepán, or making them a fair return for all they had given me. Then I fell asleep.

Nor did I take much heed of Antu, who was determined at all costs to present me with one of his wives, a child of about eight who was Lometai's sister. He had fallen for some woman the tribe had captured during a recent raid, and as the law did not allow him to take more than four wives, he had to get rid of one of the existing lot. He spent some time assuring me that he had not yet deflowered the girl, till finally, more to escape from his ceaseless importunity than anything else, I agreed to accept his gift, and took the poor thing home to live in the same hut as Urulai and myself. I saw at once that she was too young to be a real wife; so she slept with Urulai, in the big bed that had been built for me two years earlier, with animal skins spread over it, while I reverted to my *chinchorro*.

Antu at once replaced little Lay with his new woman, while Mundo (who had become more passionate than ever) spent his days out in the forest, taking his own new wife along with him. His official excuse was the urgent need to procure more meat for the tribe; but I knew that he was really engaged in a desperate search for another kadyur.

I foresaw the arrival of prospectors from all quarters, and therefore asked Mundo and Antu to issue instructions to their men to bring back to camp any persons they found out in the forest. One day I saw two colossal Negroes being led in, more dead than alive, supported by four of our Indians who had come upon them about two hours' marching distance from the village. Then Vaughan ferried in twenty assorted bums on one trip, and later I summoned them all to Pop's office and tried to make them tell me their purpose in coming. They were the absolute dregs of humanity, and I knew it; but that mattered little to me. I needed people like them, ready to risk their skins for the chance of a quick fortune; we had a common interest, their luck and mine went hand in hand. They always turned up in pairs, since this sort never travels through the jungle alone; it is rare to find them showing any courage unless driven to it by sheer necessity.

The company formed to exploit the concession was called

the Uai-parú Diamond Mining Company, of which I was both
the manager and principal shareholder. The conditions I laid
down were as follows. Each pair of prospectors was allotted a
definite area in which to work, and during their first week the
Company would supply their food on credit. Any gold or
diamonds they found would be shared fifty-fifty with the Company, and they were responsible for paying their own upkeep
from this dividend. Diamonds could be sold only to the Company, and anything they bought at the store must be paid for
in hard cash. None of them had any documents of identity, but
we entered them all on our books, with details of name, age,
birthplace, and residence: though many refused to furnish such
information, and those that did almost always falsified it.

No one complained about the conditions, either, except for
one Hungarian, who looked more intelligent than the rest and
told me he had been in a British unit during the war. He said
he had taken a look around the store and had found the prices
exorbitant: if they remained at their present level, he would
simply be working to fill my pockets and those of the *pulpero*.
Since he had no alternative, he knuckled down in the end, but
not without considerable protest.

Next day, however, I went along to see for myself. The
Hungarian was quite right, and the filibustering ex-banker took
it very hard when I told him he had to slash all his prices. He
was offering a one-bolivar bottle of rum at ten times that figure,
and a two-pound bag of flour for six bolivars, though a hun-
dredweight sack cost only twenty-five; a pair of boots worth
ten *bolos* at most he had priced up to a hundred. I fixed the
entire price tariff myself, and to avoid any extra drain on his
overheads canceled my own percentage rake-off.

There was always everything you could want in the store,
though, and the ex-banker had a hospitable side to him as well
as a shrewd business head on his shoulders. He had built a
veranda onto the store, and equipped it with tables and chairs:
this became the general camp meeting place. There was a
battery radio that could easily pick up stations such as Belém
or Manáos in Brazil, and he had also got a kerosene refrigera-
tor, which he kept permanently stocked with iced beer. But his

prices were still, on my authority, kept very high for both beer and rum.

Prospectors continued to arrive. They included Brazilians, men from the Guianas, fugitives from Cayenne, European bankrupts, and Colombian criminals wanted by the police of several countries. When the total number reached about a hundred I told Vaughan not to bring any more.

They went off on Monday morning and returned the following Saturday. Pop, the geologist, accompanied by two Taurepán tribesmen as escort, would go around inspecting their work and giving them advice. At the end of the first week they all turned up with something in their bags, and only one pair was unable to pay for the rations the Company had advanced them on arrival. That evening the whole lot of them got drunk. They danced to the music of the radio, played cards, gambled, and kept this spree up throughout Sunday.

I knew from my own experience that the area yielded industrial and commercial diamonds in approximately equal proportions, but the only good stone that turned up—a fine two-carat blue diamond—was discovered by the Hungarian and his mate. All the rest of them produced nothing but small industrial diamonds of less than a carat.

But I did not worry. I knew that no one could leave the camp except by air, since the prospect of setting off into the forest with only a week's provisions was tantamount to suicide. Furthermore, Pop made his tour of inspection every three days, and if anyone was absent from his place of work he very quickly ran him down: the Taurepán can track an *acurí* in the jungle, a creature no bigger than a rabbit. But all the same, I felt it might be a good idea to build a lockup. Any attempt to steal diamonds or gold dust would certainly lead to a brawl, granted the character of my workers and the fact that throughout Saturday and Sunday they were quite terrifyingly drunk.

On Monday morning, when they had all gone off again, bags of provisions slung from their shoulders, Vaughan arrived with fresh supplies for the store, and flew out the gold and diamonds. I got him to fly me in a lightweight aluminum canoe, fitted with a five-horsepower outboard motor. In this I could carry out a tour of inspection in one day, visiting even the most remote claims. I always took a few bottles of rum along with me, and the prospectors were delighted when I showed up.

When they returned on the Saturday I withdrew to the native village and intervened only if there was some argument over the valuation of any particular stone—a task entrusted to Pop. I generally tried to come down on the side of the prospectors—partly because they were most often in the right, and partly to keep on good terms with them and avoid the danger of creating resentful malcontents. On Monday morning I went down to see them off and wish them a good week's digging. I was the supreme authority in the camp, and it was best that I appeared only in the event of some really serious crisis, when my motives were obvious and unassailable. Otherwise I left them alone on the whole: I have never much liked being in a crowd at the best of times. Rare appearances also enhance one's authority.

At first the system worked without a hitch. It looked as though it might go on like this forever, but I sensed the unlikelihood of this, and kept alert for the slightest sign of trouble.

Chapter 13

◆

THE WAYS OF THE DIGGERS

In a very short while the camp store acquired a halo of myth as far as the Indians were concerned. Only Antu and Mundo had ever actually seen the marvels it contained, and all the rest of them spun wonderful fantasies about it in their longing and frustration.

One Monday morning, when the prospectors had gone off to work, the Indians invaded the camp—men, women, and children together—and crowded around the store, where the "talking machine" was in action. I shooed them away, but very soon, once their initial timidity had been overcome, the idea of visiting the camp during the prospectors' absence became a regular habit. I think that curiosity—second always to sexual desire—was one of their most predominant characteristics. (Not to mention the remarkable gift for ribald mimicry they possessed, which enabled them very soon to pick up the prospectors' more scurrilous phrases and expressions, and have a good idea of what they meant.) With the excuse that they needed medical attention—at the time they may even have believed it themselves—they would cross the river in their canoes, and then stand gaping in shy amazement at the goods exposed for sale. The storekeeper was at his wits' end to protect himself against their depredations. These Indians knew all about fighting and raiding, but the idea of theft was quite alien to them: they were accustomed to taking anything they found, without having to ask permission. They broke into the prospectors' huts and grabbed everything they fancied. Antu and Mundo had to exercise all their authority to recover these trophies; but neither pleas nor threats had any effect on the Taurepán, and they repeated the offense at the first possible opportunity.

I assembled the whole tribe and told them, in as simple language as possible, that they must not touch anything they found in the camp. On the other hand they could *buy* what they liked in the store. In Taurepán dialect there are no words signifying "money," "buy," or "work." With positively saintly patience, Antu at last managed to explain their meaning, and the language was promptly enriched by the addition of three loan-words from the *racionales'* tongue. Suddenly, as fast as they had been converted to religion by John Burlay, they all developed the urge to work.

I promptly selected six of the most alert tribesmen and appointed them camp guards, under Pop's command. They were armed with bows and arrows, but the tips of the arrows were only painted to look as though they were poisoned. Two more became assistant storekeepers, four got the job of sweeping out the camp and keeping the poultry yard clean, two were sent hunting, two more fishing, and another four put to work in the kitchen garden. I felt rather like Robinson Crusoe. Every Indian on the payroll received four bolivars a day. Till they learned the value of money I had, of course, to keep a strict eye on my banker-storekeeper to make sure he didn't swindle them. But even he had his work cut out. The native who gave him a ten-bolivar note for a bar of chocolate, and forgot to ask for any change, was equally likely to try to buy a carbine for the same amount, when it cost something like three hundred.

Little by little they began to correlate the satisfaction of their desires with the idea of work. Work meant that they could buy the things they wanted, like beer and rum, or sweets, or tinned food, or jackets and sombreros. The whole idea was rather a joke, really, though I found myself getting caught up in it too. For instance, when I observed this new trait in the Taurepán, I suggested to Mundo that he might do worse than

set his men building little two-seater bark canoes, and then
sell them to the prospectors.

Some of them came to understand that those small bright
shining stones could produce money for them, and they came
asking me for shovels and sieves to go prospecting themselves.
Most of them were superb swimmers, and I set them exploring
the dips in the river bed, scooping up bagfuls of gravel and
washing it through on the bank. (This latter operation they
found particularly difficult, since few of them possessed any
manual dexterity.) To begin with they used to bring me stones
that were not diamonds at all, but it did not take long for
them to learn the difference, and our total production mounted
considerably. When the other natives working for us realized
that the divers were making more than they did, the whole lot
of them wanted to look for diamonds in this fashion. I was
obliged to raise their daily wages, and I told Pop to enforce a
lower scale of payment on diamonds picked up by native
divers. I could not do without my permanent staff. If it had not
been for them the camp would very quickly have been over-
run by weeds—not to mention a plague of mice, ants, and
snakes.

I paid the Indians every Tuesday, when the prospectors
had gone. On that day the whole village invaded the camp,
and stayed there till every last cent of their wages was spent.
The whole lot, children included, got drunk. The *pulpero* had
imported a stock of Strega, and it was this liquor that most
appealed to the Indians: the moment they had two coppers to
rub together they were after it.

Now that my presence was less necessary in the camp, I
spent more time in the village. In my old hut I had a table,
some stools, and the utensils needed for rudimentary cooking.
Little Lay was growing almost visibly; and Urulai, who remained as gentle and eager to please as ever, told me it was
time I took the girl's virginity. She insisted that Lay was quite
mature enough now; but I still thought her far too young.

I had taught Urulai how to cook *spaghetti al sugo* and *risotto*
dishes. Little Lay waited on me at table. Sometimes I would

caress her, till I became thoroughly aroused; but it was always with Urulai that I satisfied this sort of desire.

As I wandered through the village I noticed things that Mundo missed, absorbed as he was in his young wife and the search for a fresh kadyur. People were becoming thoroughly idle, and got drunk with ever-increasing frequency. The women were becoming something of a delicate problem, too. On Saturdays, when the prospectors came back and went down to bathe in the river, they would hide in the bushes and watch them. The men spotted what was up, and began to make ostentatiously obscene gestures for their benefit, which excited women and children alike. They gossiped about it in the village: it became a devouring topic. If they found an excuse (which they did with increasing frequency) to visit the camp, they painted their faces like china dolls and hovered suggestively around the one or two prospectors still in camp, recovering from illnesses.

Perhaps it was just another instance of their curiosity, or perhaps they were attracted by the unfamiliar color of the men's skins—whether white or black. More probably they felt the onset of the mating season (which had already begun in the jungle) and were instinctively after a new sort of experience. Fish put on bright new nuptial scales; butterflies, snakes, and parrots changed their coats, became more colorful; the air was full of bird song, male monkeys stood guard over their harems, every beast sharpened his claws for the fray. The fox was busy digging a fresh burrow, and the night was bright with glowworms. The prospectors, most of them men between thirty and forty, full of rude health and energy, had been living lives of enforced abstinence for too long.

About twenty of them were still younger, and among these was a very effeminate fair-haired boy from Zagreb, who had teamed up with a Panamanian half-breed, a massive, oxlike fellow whose skin hinted at all the possible strains in his blood —European, Negro, Indian, even Chinese. When the men were all in camp on a Saturday they would dance with each other, and the half-breed, who was frantically jealous of his blond boy-friend, would make noisy scenes. One Sunday, when he had drunk even more than usual, he picked a quarrel with a prospector from Guiana who had danced too long with the boy; but it was not till both of them drew their machetes that the row turned into tragedy. With one stroke the half-breed severed his adversary's arm—just as the other slashed his belly open. The doctor managed to stanch the armless man's wound in time, but the half-breed became the first occupant of the graveyard down by the Uai-parú.

I sent the blond youth packing on the next plane out, and his lover followed him as soon as he was in a fit state to move. Before he left the young Yugoslav told me, in confidence, that the half-breed had hidden three diamonds of over three carats in a place which he was the only other person to know of, and demanded half their market value as the price for passing the secret on to me. I persuaded him to show me where they were, and recovered them intact. The one-armed prospector from Guiana was searched before he left, and a little tube was found concealed in his rectum containing a pair of diamonds, one of six carats, the other of two.

Cases of homosexuality began to increase at an alarming rate. There was one quite revolting affair, straight out of a casebook of sexual psychopathology, which obliged me to expel the Hungarian; but this was by no means the most serious episode.

One day an Indian woman approached Pop and tried to sell him four small diamonds, averaging half a carat apiece. Pop detained the woman and asked me to interrogate her. She was the wife of one of the official camp hunters, neither a young nor an attractive woman any longer, but still extremely lascivious. She often went down to the river with the other women to watch the prospectors bathing. Her husband was a great deal older than she was, and had three other much younger wives.

"Where did you find these diamonds?" I asked her.

The woman made no reply. The Taurepán were quite incapable of making up lies on the spur of the moment.

"Did your husband give you them?"

She shook her head.

"If you don't tell me, I shall be forced to have a word with your husband."

There was silence for a moment or two. Then the woman, eyes fixed on the ground, confessed that she had been given them by two prospectors, one white and one Negro, who worked the same stretch of river, not far outside the village.

"Why did they give you these diamonds?"

"I went into the forest and met them there."

"You know what to expect if the men of your tribe find out you have been going with a man who is not your husband?"

"Yes."

"You won't go off to meet any more prospectors then, will you?"

I called to Pop, made him give her a few bolivars, and sent her packing. Then I got in a canoe and went down to see the men responsible, and tried to point out to them what would happen if the natives found out what was going on. They raised the usual excuses: no other women were available, and anyway these native women kept enticing them.

"Sure, they're pretty rough," one of them told me, "but seeing as how they're all that's going—"

"All right," I said, "skip it. And one other thing—diamonds are shared with the Company, fifty-fifty. You can't give them away as presents."

I knew there was only one solution to this problem, but I felt I must talk it over with Antu first.

"My workmen need women," I told him.

"There are no women here for them," Antu said firmly.

"I know. That's why I'm thinking of bringing some in from outside."

Antu thought this over for a moment.

"But then," he objected, "*my* men will become quite uncontrollable—what do you think will happen when they catch a glimpse of these new women of yours?"

He had a point there, and no mistake.

One evening Tommasino appeared on the threshold of my

hut, just before supper-time. Since we had not yet had our meal I told Urulai to set a place for him, too.

He was an odd creature, of middling height, with a bull-neck, an enormous beard, and thick chestnut-colored hair; it seemed he had been a farmer all his life. His expression was by no means amiable, and his manners were worse, though he had some thoughts and ideas about life that he might have picked up in books. He always looked as though he felt utter scorn and contempt for his surroundings.

"You're lucky," he told me. "You've got two women looking after you. What d'you want with two, anyway?"

"All the rest of them have four," I replied, without thinking. In this, as in so many things, I instinctively aligned myself with the Indians. Then I added, pulling myself up: "Anyway, can't you see that one of them's a mere child?"

"Some have too much, some have nothing," Tommasino mumbled. "If she's too young for you, why don't you turn her over to me?"

"Look, Tommasino, come to the point. What are you after?"

"I need a woman," he said. "I'll even marry one of these Indian girls if I have to. You've got to find me a woman or give me a week's leave in Ciudad Bolívar."

"That's out of the question. We need you here, and your contract is for two years. There aren't any spare Indian women, in any case."

"There's one: Mundo's fifth."

He was quite right. Counting his new young wife (the one acquired on a raid), Mundo now had a harem of five.

"But do you like Indian women?"

"I like any women," he said.

The next day I raised the matter with Mundo and Antu. It was by no means easy to persuade them. The witch doctor was even more obdurate; but I knew that Tommasino would eventually win him over, with a few tins of sardines and a bottle of rum. The wife whom Mundo thus relinquished was in fact a very ordinary sort of woman, neither ugly nor a beauty, and about twenty-two years old—by which time Taurepán women are generally past their prime. The wedding, according to custom, could not be held till the time of the full moon.

That had got Tommasino fixed up, but what about the rest of them? Whether Antu liked it or not, I would have to fly in some tarts. When Vaughan landed with the next load of supplies, I asked him to dig out four women prepared to come back with him to the Uai-parú and ply their trade among a hundred diamond prospectors.

"Tell them there's one thing they can be sure of," I said. "They'll make a packet."

Vaughan assured me the proposition was a feasible one, and promised to bring the girls back on his next trip. Then I had a discussion with Pop, Tommasino, and the doctor, Beato, about the best way to organize the women. Meanwhile we chose a site for a new barrack-hut—well away from the others—and fitted it up with four separate rooms and four baths, so that the women could wash between clients. Tommasino instantly christened this building "La Casa de las Putas": "whorehouse" sounds better in Spanish.

But the problem of accommodation was a minor matter in comparison with the danger of V.D. The doctor would of course examine the women as soon as they arrived; but there were about a hundred men in camp, and most of them, before they joined us, had been roving the jungle as *mineros de libre aprovechamiento*, or free-lance prospectors. Whenever they visited one of the shack townships rapidly springing up in the districts where diamonds were to be found, they wanted a woman in their hammock: Indian or Negro, young or old, it made no difference, and they cared little about hygienic or any other precautions. Even supposing they all showed a clean bill of health at present, it might well be that some of them had had inadequate treatment and were not properly cured. We were not equipped with a pathological laboratory, and Beato already had more work on his hands than he could cope with: the ten beds in the infirmary were almost always occupied. The most prevalent complaints were malarial fevers and Leishman's disease, a tropical malady caused by a certain parasite that attacks the skin and mucous membranes. On top of all this the witch doctor, with considerable shrewdness, very soon began consulting Beato over his own patients in the village.

We would have to take a nurse on as well, it seemed. The situation promised to be a complicated one. But I could not allow the men to go on having sexual relations with one another.

About this time Antu went off on a hunting expedition to procure enough fresh meat for the feast at Tommasino's wedding. The ceremony was, as always, a most important one. Everything was running smoothly in the camp, and I decided to accompany Antu myself. We set off at dawn along a small track beside the river. Antu marched at the head of the column, I was directly behind him, and every other able-bodied male in the tribe followed on in the rear. Dogs ran hither and thither, but there was no barking. The absence of game struck me as odd. I asked Antu about it.

"Animals don't like men," he told me, in the slightly resentful voice he always employed when referring to my work. "Men are their enemies. You have put men all along the river. These men shoot at anything they see. Animals prefer to be left alone in peace."

But finally the dogs set up a great barking about fifty yards in front of us, and then one of them let out a great yelp of anguish: a huge amphibious snake had caught him by one leg and was dragging him down to the river. Antu dropped his gun, grabbed a machete, and with one clean stroke severed the serpent's head from its body. It sank into the water, still clutching the wretched dog, its mutilated body looping and writhing like a whip. Two Indians dived in and rescued the dog, which had the snake's monstrous head clamped fast to its leg. Two others meanwhile lashed a liana around the reptile's still quivering body, and hauled it up over the branch of a tree as though on a pulley. A third man sat astride the branch, made a circular incision in the skin, grabbed hold of it, slipped off the branch, and slid all the way down to the ground, peeling off the skin like a glove as he went. The serpent was then chopped up and its flesh wrapped up in palm leaves for the journey back to the village. The Indians regarded it as a great delicacy. It was a young *habomá*, already over twenty feet in length, and nearly two in diameter at its thickest part. When fully grown this creature is capable of swallowing a stag or a wild boar.

That day we reached the southernmost Taurepán village, whose inhabitants made a specialty of growing yuca, and where the headman was the father both of Lometai and of my young wife Lay. I had remembered to bring them some presents from the camp store; but, these small novelties excepted, the community preserved all those traditional characteristics which our main village had lost through contact with the white man.

After a two hours' march we turned westward and presently reached a high plateau. Hundreds of brightly colored parrots were visible under the palm trees; the troupials were singing everywhere, and nearer the ground fluttered great clouds of sheeny dark-blue butterflies. High in the tallest *guaramánes* brown and white squirrels scuttled out of sight as we approached. Just above our heads the iguanas nibbled on at their leaves, quite unperturbed by our presence.

For a good hour we plodded on along the same grassy track, through the same immutable forest scene. Though the sun was still high, under that arching vault of foliage it quickly became dark. Antu therefore split us up into three parties. Five of the Indians and I, all armed with carbines, were to stay put. The other two groups, each of ten men, were to go on ahead with the dogs, fanning out on either side of the track, for a further three or four miles. In the morning they would come back in extended line, beating the undergrowth, and driving the game in our direction.

When dawn broke, Antu selected a tree for each of us to climb in readiness. We did not see much, however. The first creature to arrive was a large bird resembling an ostrich: it fell transfixed by two arrows. Next came a female *chigüire*, but it was pregnant, and Antu motioned us to let it go. Our subse-

quent bag included a brace of roebuck, a tapir, and the larger
part of a herd of wild pigs. By now the forest was in a deafen-
ing uproar, with wounded animals, hysterical parrots, and
other terrified birds all contributing to the general clamor.
When the noise finally died away we clambered down from
our trees and set about skinning and quartering the animals
we had killed.

The following afternoon we got back to the village, just in
time for the full moon and Tommasino's wedding to his Indian
bride. Vaughan arrived bright and early next morning, but
without any prostitutes. When he heard about the feast he
decided to stay on for it.

The actual ceremony that Tommasino went through was the
same as I had undergone. Tommasino, however, had "done
things properly," with as much care as he would have ex-
pended on impressing the neighbors back home. His bride
had gold bracelets on her ankles and wrists, gold pendants
in her ears, a gold torque around her neck. Her breasts were
draped in muslin, and her features liberally adorned with
rouge, lipstick, and blue eye-shadow. The whole thing looked
like a scene from a film.

A lot had changed since my own wedding to Lolomai. Then I
was the only white man there, and dressed as the Taurepán
did. But now not only were the group of Europeans—Tommasino, Vaughan, Beato, and Pop—dressed in Western clothes,
but the whole tribe too: and very ridiculous they looked in
their ill-fitting, unaccustomed finery. They had learned to
smoke, which they did with much awkward spluttering. When
the ceremony was over they all began to souse themselves
with rum and lukewarm beer as well as *cachire.* In a very short
while they were hopelessly drunk.

I found the spectacle unbearably depressing; and Antu, too,
looked worried by it. The cheerful, carefree people I had
known, so fond of dancing and *cachire,* had been transformed
into a band of nasty drunks, spewing and quarreling without
any dignity or self-restraint.

Nor could I blind myself to the fact that I was responsible
for all this, that my determination to make a fortune had

inevitably led to it. When I was sowing potatoes up in the Andes I worked hard myself and made my peons do likewise: I was never conscious of the passage of time, and even my moments of utter exhaustion were lightened by hopes of the harvest to come. Now my energies were devoted to organizing and running the camp. I fixed the price of diamonds, rationed out food supplies, and brought in women. I lived for a tomorrow that never seemed to come. From time to time I went back to the village, rather like someone going down to his country cottage for the weekend.

The Taurepáns' previous existence had been wretched enough, without defense against illness, and scarcely better equipped to cope with famine; but they always lived in the present, that immutable present they had cherished for hundreds of years. They had the bare minimum of laws and customs needed to keep such a small community united; and since they remained closely bound to the forest, and natural life in general, they did not regard those laws as binding or permanent. Within fairly elastic limits they were always ready to change or abolish the rules of the game; as a system it had a touch of perfection about it. Now, even if I managed to save them from syphilis and alcoholism, and to cure them too of their parasitical diseases, I could not prevent them from learning to work today so that in a week's time they could buy something they did not need.

But what was done was done, and could not be changed. I went to bed. Before I fell asleep I found myself wondering why I still remained hesitant about initiating Lay into the pleasures of womanhood. To judge from her physical appearance, and the way she looked at me sometimes, she was more than ready by now.

But in the days that followed I had no time for such reflections.

Chapter 14

◆

LAS PUTAS

An unforgettable episode: the arrival *de las putas,* the Whores'
Invasion. The airstrip lay on the right bank of the river, the
same side as the village. The moment they heard the throb of
motors in the sky, everyone left what they were doing and ran
to see the "great bird" descend. The spectacle had lost none of
its fascination with time.

That morning only Antu knew what was in the wind.
Vaughan got out first, and the women followed him. There
were four of them: a tall, imposing near-white girl, two mulattoes wearing hats trimmed with flowers and cherries, and a
Negress. All four were dressed up as though they'd just stepped
through their front door onto a city sidewalk. They clambered
down, their curiosity tempered with a certain amount of surprise and alarm at the sight of all these laughing Indians
crowding in on them. When the first two appeared, the Taurepán, who had never seen anything so gaudily done up in their
lives, stood paralyzed with amazement. Then, as though at
some unseen signal, they rushed on the new arrivals, the
women leading the way. An Indian girl made for one of the
mulattoes, and snatched off her hat. This was the prelude to a
general attack.

The four wretched tarts found themselves at the center of
a furious crowd, threatened by innumerable outstretched arms
and hands that were clearly determined to strip off every last
stitch of clothing they possessed. They defended themselves
as best they could, kicking, punching, and scratching vigor-

ously: one of them tried to clamber back into the aircraft, but someone grabbed her by the ankle and hauled her down again. By now the men were mixed up in the fray as well. I kept yelling at them to stop it; Mundo was splitting his sides with laughter. Finally Vaughan had a bright idea: he unslung his rifle and fired five shots in the air.

This brought Mundo back to his senses. Urged on by me, he strode into the melee, placing himself between the four women and their assailants, and gradually managed to restore some sort of order. At this point Antu came hurrying up, and did his best to soothe down the women's angry curiosity as well as the growing lasciviousness of the men. The tarts, weeping, bedraggled, and practically naked, begged us to put them back aboard the plane and take them away, anywhere. Meanwhile the Indians capered around, giggling and waving their various trophies—shoes, pairs of briefs, slips, bras, torn scraps of material.

We did our best to make the tarts look decent again—we even lent them our shirts—and then we bundled them aboard the canoe (accompanied by lewd hoots of delight from the entire tribe) and ferried them across to the far side of the river, where Pop and Tommasino were waiting to take them to their hut. Here, after finding all their luggage still intact and drinking a cup of coffee each, they soon began to perk up again, and launched into a flood of obscene invective against the natives and their womenfolk.

"That's why you're over here," I told them. "This is your private hut. A room for each of you, and running water. The kitchen's outside."

The prospectors had left at crack of dawn, not knowing that the women were arriving later that morning. The only men left in camp were the doctor, the storekeeper, Pop, Tommasino, and the native guards. The latter stared till their eyes popped, but did nothing else except point at the tarts' complexions, and giggle. They found the white girl's bleached hair and ample curves quite hilarious.

Half an hour or so later the four women came down to my office.

"What's your name?" I asked the near-white.

The answer came in a rapid singsong: "My name is Maria, I come from Lara *estado* near Acarigua, twenty-five years of age, profession, prostitute."

The Negress, Josephine, was an attractive creature, with small firm breasts and a sensuous mouth. She was born in Ciudad Bolívar, and was twenty-three. The two mulattoes, Dorothy and Catherine, had emigrated from Port of Spain to be chambermaids in Caracas.

I told them the camp rules, fixed their rate at twenty bolivars a time, and advised them to be on the lookout for V.D. among their clients. The doctor had put an adequate ration of permanganate solution at their disposal, and the storekeeper would advance them goods on credit for the first week.

"And above all," I said, "*no Indians*. They've all got wives, and I don't want any trouble."

But at that stage the admonition seemed superfluous. The thought of so much as seeing an Indian still filled them with terror.

Then I escorted them across to the infirmary for their medical check-up. We had to pass through the "ward," where their appearance provoked the patients to considerable enthusiasm.

"*Hay muchachas!*" they called. "*Arriba las muchachas!*" Someone waved a dirty handkerchief like a flag.

The doctor examined them in turn: Maria first, then Dorothy and Catherine, and finally Josephine, whose interview lasted a good deal longer. As I have already remarked, the doctor was twenty-seven, and a Spaniard.

That evening the store closed early. The ex-banker spent the night with Maria, Pop slept with Catherine, and the doctor had another go at his Negress.

The next day, Tuesday, was the day when the Indians brought their diamonds for valuation. They were accompanied by their wives, who then helped them to spend their earnings in the store.

The guards did all they could to keep this crowd clear of the hut belonging to the four women, who had wisely barricaded themselves inside. To satisfy the natives' natural curiosity I invited them to make a tour of the camp, with the guards escorting them. The women and children soon got used to the place, and gradually quieted down. But the men had been drinking, and knew what they wanted. I had to lock the tarts' door. Antu was not there; he never visited the camp on a Tuesday. I called to Mundo, who had obviously got a good skinful aboard himself, and patiently explained to him that he must take his people back to the village earlier than usual.

"I want the white woman," was Mundo's only comment.

"You've got four wives already, all to yourself. These women are for the diggers, who haven't any of their own. This way they won't go after *your* women any more. You must tell your people to leave them alone."

"Very well. But *I* am not people. I am the headman. I want the white woman."

I was obliged to be extremely diplomatic with Mundo— something that I had not done for a long while. And it took more diplomacy than usual to make him abandon this idea and go back to the village with all his subjects.

On Saturday morning the diggers began straggling in, and before lunch-time they were all back. No sooner had the news of the tarts' arrival got out—and the word spread like wildfire —than they were all down besieging the brothel, unwashed and unshaven, before they even turned in their diamonds for valuation. The poor girls had a hard time of it for the next two days and nights. On both Saturday and Sunday I had to shut the brothel at midnight, officially, to let them get a few hours' sleep. Some of the diggers even went back on Monday morning, before setting off for work.

A short while afterward the Negress and the white girl were strolling around the camp as though nothing had happened. But the two Trinidad mulattoes didn't stir from their beds, and had to be visited by the doctor.

Previously the diggers had never come back during the week, unless they were ill or had an accident. But now any excuse would serve, and the reason was always the same: the *casa de las putas.*

Catherine was the first of them to leave the brothel. Pop had fallen for her and wanted to have her to himself; and she was only too glad to move out of the big hut and give up her exhausting weekend *corvée*. She moved in with Pop and thereafter became the perfect wife: she even demanded a sewing machine, and began to run up clothes for the Indian women and their children. Next it was Maria's turn, bleached hair and all: she set up house with the *pulpero,* and became a prosperous, respectable storekeeper's wife. She was born to stand behind a counter: it was her natural vocation. Dorothy went off with Angelo, a young Italian boy who worked a claim along the river, together with two companions. I went around to see him some days later: the mulatto was having a busy and enjoyable time, washing shirts in the river, singing happily, cooking meals, and sleeping with all three of them. The only one now left in the "big hut" was Josephine, the Negress. She gritted her teeth and stuck it out: she must have saved a small fortune. But in fact her motive was not covetousness; I only discovered the real reason later. The guard commander in the camp was a youth of twenty called Marubu, a great friend of Antu's. Josephine had fallen in love with him, and used to let him in secretly at night, when everyone was asleep. Marubu was married to two Indian girls, sisters, whose combined ages did not come to more than twenty; but he had lost his head about the Negress. (She probably introduced him to more spicy pleasures than his girl-wives knew about.) He wanted to marry her, if Josephine would agree to come and live in the village with the other two. He was eaten up with jealousy and wanted to stop the diggers from coming anywhere near her.

Antu tried to dissuade him, and failed. Then he sent the witch doctor around to see him.

"Canaima has entered into your body, my son," the Sapulí told him. "Go back to your village. I will help you to fight Canaima, and Mauri will be with you once again. You will live happily with your wives forever after."

But the possessed Marubu, far from fighting Canaima, sent his two wives back to their father (who was not overdisturbed by this move, since he could easily find another bidder for

them), gave up his job as guard commander, and went off
with Josephine to live in a hut he had built beside a remote
stream, well away from the village and the camp. There he
began to prospect for diamonds, and the only time I saw him
in camp was when he came to sell diamonds or buy supplies
at the store. He never brought Josephine with him.

Now the "big hut" was deserted, and the diggers were beginning to complain. I imported a new batch of women, and
indeed I had to be replacing them continually, since in a very
short time all of them settled down, each with one man. The
diggers built a rough sort of hut near their working site (a
few bamboo stakes, a palm-leaf roof: a *tarimba*, in fact) and
then had their women along with them. The women worked as
hard as the men did, sometimes harder.

But it was the Indians who gave me cause for concern. At
an early stage in his relationship with Josephine, Marubu
must have passed on among his fellow tribesmen some of the
tricks he had learned in bed with the Negress. Now all of
them wanted to have a "foreign woman," whether she was
white or not. Marubu had set a precedent, and now there was
no holding them. Every time a new batch of women arrived,
the Indians went straight around to the brothel with their
twenty bolivars. The tarts got used to the idea quickly
enough, and the Indians' wives said nothing. They saw their
husbands march into the "big hut," waited outside till they
had finished, and then—if there was any money left over—
went off to the store with them.

Some of them, however, got their own back: when they
went out in the morning to search the forest for roots and
berries, grubs, lizards, and the like, they would drift in the
direction of the huts where the still unattached diggers lived,
and it did not take much persuasion on their part to make the
men give them what they wanted.

Antu, who was the only really sensible person in the whole
tribe, saw all this, and chafed with impotent rage. Another
Indian had now followed Marubu's example. One day Antu
came and begged me not to bring in any more women. About

twenty of them had now settled down in happy domesticity; four remained, but it would, I fancied, not be long before they found their soul mates, too. I promised Antu that when this happened, the *casa de las putas* would be closed once and for all.

A few days later the doctor informed me that he had a case in the infirmary that rather worried him. The man had been running a high temperature for two days, and clearly was suffering from malaria. He was a Colombian from Barranquilla, called Francisco Otiz; he had recently brought in a sizable stone, and seemed very pleased with life. He had 2850 bolivars banked with the Company, the fruit of many months' hard work. He was a natural optimist, always brimming over with enthusiasm: if things failed to go well for him one day, well, then tomorrow he would make a new start somewhere else, open up the ground, dig out tons of shale that had lain untouched for thousands of years, and in it he'd find the biggest diamond ever, a new Cullinan.* And if he drew a blank tomorrow, doubtless his number would come up the day after that, or some time. By fostering such hopes a digger can always turn them into certainties in his own mind.

He died that night without regaining consciousness. On Saturday we all followed his coffin to the cemetery, and Pop read a few verses from his shabby old Bible at the graveside.

Next Saturday one prospector, and his woman, failed to show up. They were frequently late back: they never liked leaving any loose shale unwashed. But this time they were still missing on Sunday, and on Monday morning I set out in search of them, taking one Indian with me. We followed the stream where they worked, and after a while spotted the vultures circling overhead, always in the same place. Then we heard the feeble whining of a dog. We reached the hut and found it deserted, the fire black and cold. Finally the howling dog guided us to the right place—the actual hole where they had been digging. Its walls had collapsed, burying the poor wretches: only their arms were visible. The dog

* This famous stone, of 3035 carats, was found in a South African mine.

was at the end of its tether, but still managing to keep the vultures at bay.

The woman had gone off with this particular digger only a fortnight before. Before she left she told me she thanked the *Virgen* she had come here, because at last she had found her man. She was a Colombian, from La Cruz. Tommasino discovered a little tube of diamonds hidden between her breasts, and this led me to dig out the hole and explore it further. The unfortunate pair had, in fact, stumbled on a first-rate seam: a small fortune lay hidden there.

A similar accident befell Pierre, a French fugitive from Cayenne. I learned his story in bits and pieces, between glasses of beer: how he had struggled headlong through swampy jungle, with men and dogs in hot pursuit of him; how he had first sought asylum in Dutch Guiana, and then—to avoid the possibility of extradition—in Venezuela, the "Land of Liberty" as he always called it. He had found a magnificent blue diamond of eleven carats. His companion, who had gone off to fetch some water, heard him screaming for help, rushed back, and saw him lying in a pool of his own blood, trying to defend himself against the raking claws of a big ocelot. He dared not shoot, for fear of hitting Pierre. When he finally managed to drive the big cat off with a blow of his rifle butt, it was too late. The French boy died a few minutes later.

Another Saturday one of the prospectors came back on his own and said that his companion, a Mexican called Brito, had gone off into the forest and vanished. Some days later he came to me and said he wanted to pack up and leave. I told him he was perfectly within his rights, and could do so.

On Monday we ferried him and his luggage across the river to where the plane was waiting; but instead of putting him aboard, we took him into a nearby hut and searched him. Concealed in the lining of his grip we found no less than twelve stones, including two fifteen-carat ones. I asked him why he had not turned them in. The fellow hung his head and made no reply. Then he launched into the usual hard-luck story. "I've got my children and my old mother to think of. I

wanted to take them something—they've no one but me to
look after them—"

"If you sold the stones without any certificate of origin
you wouldn't get much more than we're offering."

"I don't know why I did it, I don't really," he muttered. And
then: "Maybe it was because they were so lovely."

They were, indeed, magnificent diamonds.

"All right," I said, "I'll pay you for them. But first you're
going to tell me what you did to Brito. Otherwise you don't
get a cent."

"I don't know anything, I tell you. I looked for him, but he
never came back, he never showed up again. I swear on my
children's heads that I know nothing. Don't give me any
money, keep the diamonds, but please, I beg of you, let me
go back to my children—"

He swore by his children, by his old mother, by the Holy
Virgin and Christ crucified; and all the time big tears were
rolling down his cheeks.

I nodded to Tommasino. One of the Indians gripped his
arms and twisted them up behind his back, two others pulled
his legs apart, while another two twisted a long strip of cloth
around his testicles and stood one on either side of him, each
holding an end of it. They began to pull.

"If you don't talk," I said, "they'll pull harder. And harder."

I went out of the hut and left the two Indians to get on with
it. The man's screams nearly shattered my eardrums, but they
didn't last for long.

Some readers may perhaps object to the method by which I
made this digger talk; but I knew him to be a violent man and
a chronic liar. When I found so many diamonds on him, I
was convinced that my suspicions had been well founded. I
only hoped I might prove to be in time to save Brito.

After a little while Tommasino came out and told me the
fellow had made a full confession. When I went in he flung
himself on his knees before me and swore that Brito had tried
to murder him, but he'd been too quick, he'd struck Brito
first, in self-defense. He also told me where he had hidden the

body: it was at the bottom of a river pool, with two large rocks to weight it down.

The fish had picked poor Brito clean: only his skeleton was left when we got there.

Shortly after this Angelo was pinned under a heavy boulder while levering it away from a particularly rich seam. Beato was obliged to amputate his foot. With Angelo *hors de combat*, his two mates decided to call it a day. Catherine, the mulatto who lived with the three of them, shed a few tears (she was an affectionate girl, and quite fond of them) but a few days later was shacked up again, this time with a gigantic Negro; the Negro was enormously flattered at getting her.

One morning I was wakened soon after dawn by a series of shots coming from the camp. Antu and Tommasino had also heard them and were hastening down toward the river. We thought the camp must have been attacked; and indeed so it had, but not quite in the way we supposed. Thousands of parrots had descended on our precious kitchen garden, and were devouring it wholesale. Pop, his woman, the storekeeper, and the nurse were all banging away on empty oil drums, but this had no more effect than shooting had done. Antu at once told them it was a pure waste of time. Now they had discovered our patches of Indian corn they would certainly return the following day, even if they failed to consume the entire crop here and now.

All the labor that had gone into cultivating the kitchen garden was wasted: on every bed there squatted three, sometimes four parrots. Our lettuces had been eaten by grasshoppers, mice and rats had accounted for the potatoes, and the tomatoes had never come up. The natives were obviously right to eschew cultivation and rely on whatever they could pick up in the forest.

The concession was paying off handsomely, but everything else had turned sour on me. I was not sorry that the rainy season was nearly due, with its enforced leisure: long idle days that I could spend in the village, away from the confusion and violence of the camp.

Chapter 15

♦

HUNTING THE KADYUR

The dog I had found guarding its dead master against vultures
—though itself almost at death's door—was called Siskuss,
which is Taurepán for "thunderbolt." It was a heavy-
shouldered, muscular beast, with a long shaggy coat and a
surprising turn of speed. It had taken an extravagant liking
to me, and tended to follow me wherever I went. It never
allowed itself to be sidetracked from my scent by that of a
fox or a *lapa:* this, I fancy, must have cost it quite an effort.
It was, I am sure, its resemblance to Kaicusé—rubbed in by its
constant presence—that set me brooding over the old days at
Diamond Mountain, when Lolomai was still alive. Pop and
Tommasino ran the camp and the business with admirable
efficiency, and could get on very well without any help on
my part. Why not go off again for a while?

I had no trouble selling the idea to Antu. He was even more
eager than I was to get away from the diggers' camp and all
the trouble it involved him in, and to forget, for a while at
least, the humiliation of not being able to lift a finger to prevent the evils that were befalling his people. Mundo was
still village chief—though now, with the witch doctor as his
amiable boon companion, he got hopelessly drunk every
evening.

We took the canoe with paddles instead of the motorized
one, and set off, accompanied by Siskuss. As usual, the whole
village turned out on the riverbank to see us off. We stopped

at various points along the river to exchange a word or two with the diggers as we passed them, and on the evening of the second day reached the hut where Marubu and Josephine lived—the most isolated couple in the whole community. Beyond them there were no other human beings for literally hundreds of miles. Finally we found ourselves back in the peace of the forest again, with no other men around us, just as it had been before. We seldom spoke; if either of us wished to draw the other's attention to anything, we communicated by gestures. Instinctively we took care to keep our paddle strokes in time. The canoe glided smoothly along, close to the bank, brushing the overhanging branches. Those little caymans which the Brazilians call *yacaré* and the Venezuelans *baba* dived into the water at our approach. A kingfisher fluttered ahead of us, rending the air with a strident whistling cry every time we drew near him. Hundreds of bats hung from the boughs above us, and snakes lay in wait on the banks, watching for rats and iguanas to come down and drink. Once we glimpsed a solitary monkey, a tiny creature with an enormous tail and off-white face, which Antu called a *sukwiky*. It amused itself by flinging a series of sticks and turds at us, but never managed to score a direct hit.

On a bough projecting far out over the water I spotted a *pereza* monkey, very comfortably settled. I poked him with an arrow to see if I could scare him, but he seemed hardly aware of my presence. Nor did he look put out when the dog began barking and snarling at him, teeth bared. Having munched his way along the branch he was on, he glanced up at the next one overhead, cocked an eye at us for a moment, and then decided to make the effort and jump. One tree can last these creatures a week; once he has eaten it bare of foliage he can't be bothered to move on, it's too exhausting, so he just puts his head between his back legs and rolls down the trunk like a furry ball. Whether the *pereza* feels fear or not I do not know; but it certainly remains sublimely indifferent to any sort of danger, including wild beasts (which eat it) and human beings.

One afternoon, when the sun was still fairly high, I decided to climb to the top of a hill we could see from the river. It was a slow and exhausting ascent, since we had to hack our way through the undergrowth with machetes, and clamber over various large boulders that blocked our path. But when we reached the summit the view was unparalleled: a vast sea of treetops, blown this way and that by the wind, and revealing the most varied and unexpected hues. Then, suddenly, the dog began to bark. We found him standing outside the entrance to some sort of lair beneath a rock, hair bristling. Antu studied the ground and assured me that the creature was certainly not a member of the cat family. Since these retreats normally have more than one exit, he was just going around the rock to make a thorough check when some black object darted out about ten yards away from us, fast as an arrow, and vanished into the forest.

"*Kadyur!*" Antu gasped, and at once sicked the dog on after it.

To me the idea of pursuing an animal through the heart of the jungle with only one dog seemed completely lunatic; but Antu must know better than I could which risks were feasible and which not. Besides, the idea of capturing a kadyur attracted me: not because I wanted to try another dose (I had had quite enough of that already) but to have the beast analyzed, bones and all, since it obviously contained some substance that many people would regard as a good deal more precious than diamonds.

"We'll never catch it!" I shouted to Antu.

He was already well ahead of me. "It's a night hunting animal," he called. "It won't get away from the dog. If the dog catches it, he'll keep it pinned down till we get there."

The barking was fading away into the distance now, and we had to force our way through an increasingly dense tangle of cactus, lianas, dwarf palms, iriarteas, and heaven knows what else. Finally, when for about the tenth time I had firmly repressed the urge to lie down somewhere, in the first clear patch of ground I could find, I heard the dog bark again, but loud and clear now, and much closer.

"He's got it!" Antu exclaimed, and shot off at the double.

But he failed to notice a huge wasps' nest that was hanging from a branch overhead, and ran full tilt into it. The wasps were all over us before we realized what had happened. Our only chance was to retreat along the path we had come by, which was at least clear.

"Your eyes!" Antu shouted. "Look out for your eyes!"

But by shielding my eyes I became unable to see where I was going, with the result that I stumbled and fell. The wasps swarmed all over me. I remembered having glimpsed a vast bunch of *cortaderia* ahead of me, a plant with serrated spear-like leaves, sharp-edged as razors. To land in the *cortaderia* after being mobbed by wasps would be needless masochism.

The furious insects pursued us back down the big ridge we had come along, and only drew off when we plunged into the jungle itself. Every exposed portion of my body was excruciatingly painful, and my face was rapidly swelling up. We were a long way from the river. I rolled over on the ground as dogs do to scratch an itch on their back, but this gave me no appreciable relief. My eyes were so puffy that they closed up.

Antu had suffered just as much as I had, but I fancy he felt the pain rather less; at all events, he went on talking. The dog's barks were still audible.

"You won't be able to see at all soon," Antu remarked. He propped me up against a tree trunk and placed a carbine and machete beside me.

With darkness came silence: I may even have lost consciousness. We had neither food nor water, but I kept telling myself that an Indian does not die of thirst or hunger in the forest. I was most disappointed at not having got a good look at the legendary kadyur.

After what seemed an eternity—I was still virtually blind—I heard Antu's voice, and felt the dog's tongue licking my swollen face.

"Water," I croaked.

Antu took me by the hand and led me under a big hanging liana. With one blow of his machete he severed it, and water streamed down over my face. I drank all I could catch—little enough, since a liana, for all its size, contains no more than half a pint of water.

"How are you managing?" I asked Antu.

"I can only see out of one eye. But we'll be all right again quite soon."

When the wasps attacked us Antu had deliberately sacrificed one eye so that he could see where he was running. He covered the other one up, and it had remained unharmed.

"What about the kadyur?"

"It was a female," Antu said. "I let it go."

For two days after that I could not see, and ran a temperature.

One day, as we were rounding a bend in the river, we saw a curious sight on the bank: about fifty monkeys, sitting there like so many souls in Purgatory, while across the river the leader of the band gesticulated and screeched furiously at them, like a temperamental conductor. Then, as we watched, one of the monkeys clambered down into the water, then another, clinging with his front paws to the first one's tail, and after him a third, who repeated the pattern—and so, eventually, they all were afloat, the young ones clinging to their mothers' necks. They formed an elongated chain, which stretched right across the river in the teeth of the current. When they reached dry land again the monkeys shook the water from themselves and all began to converse in guttural screechings. Then a sad wailing noise arose on the near side of the river: in the confusion one small ape had been left behind on our bank, and its mother was incapable of swimming back to fetch it. Antu jumped ashore and rescued it. As we paddled across to the other side I thought it might be rather fun to keep the little creature, and bring it up with other human babies in the village—always supposing we could find an Indian woman to wet-nurse it, which was by no means impossible. But then I realized this was a characteristically European idea, and dropped it. We put the baby ape ashore on the same side as the main body, and instantly its mother snatched it up, hugged it to her, and, still chattering, shot to the top of the nearest tree in sight.

Another morning we were aroused by the dog barking. We peered out, but in the feeble dawn light could not discern any reason for Siskuss's excitement and alarm. It was Antu who spotted it, a split second before he put his bare foot down on the ground: the advance guard of a great column of ants had just passed by, and the main body was due at any moment.

We grabbed the few possessions we had brought ashore for the night (my mosquito boots had already been invaded) and ran for it. We were only five yards or so from the river, but in that distance the ants managed to bite me all over my feet and calves. The canoe was moored to an overhanging branch, but Antu reckoned it would be safer to tie up to a rock in midstream. We did so, and settled down to watch.

For over two hours millions af ants marched by, in a tight-packed column no more than a yard wide. Antu could not explain the reason for this mass migration: it was the first time he had ever seen such a phenomenon himself. But he remembered having heard tales from old men in the tribe about devastating hordes of rats and ants on the move.

A little way off the ants' chosen route was barred by a stream. We overtook the advance guard and in half an hour reached this watercourse, which was about twelve feet wide at the point where it flowed into the main river. The ants arrived ten minutes later, swarmed down the bank, and then— as though in response to an order—wheeled smartly to the left and proceeded along the line of the stream. The main body did not even reach the bank, but left-wheeled a yard before it, and followed the advance guard. I now observed that they carried with them sticks, dry leaves, and bits of foliage, in larger or smaller groups according to the weight of the object. It was as though the earth itself were in motion.

They advanced for several hundred yards, and then assaulted the stream on a fifty-yard-wide front, at a point where the water ran shallower and less fast. They plunged into the water, clinging with their front legs to the sticks and leaves they had brought with them, swimming frantically with their rear legs in an effort to reach the farther shore. Many, as was bound to happen, were swept away and gobbled up by the fish, which swarmed to the spot in a flash. Nevertheless, millions of them got across successfully. When we beat our hasty retreat only the advance guard had got ashore. The ground that this myriad horde had passed over was flattened to a depth of about an inch and a half, as though it had been traversed by an army of dwarfs.

We had to make another stop because of Siskuss, who was all set to have a fight with a snake. The snake lay coiled up still, but its head was erect, ready to strike.

"It's just finished eating," Antu said, pointing to a great swelling in the reptile's body. "Nasty sort of snake, that one. Best to kill it."

I blew its head off with one shot from my carbine. Then, while I held the truncated carcass firmly stretched out, Antu slit up its belly. There emerged an enormous iguana, somewhat dazed but still very much alive. It tottered off slowly toward the nearest tree, and tried to climb up it, but was too weak to keep its foothold. We left it to make out as best it could—though Siskuss had other ideas on the subject.

That same day the dog saved our lives. Inquisitive as always, he unearthed a gigantic black spider just by the place where we were rigging up our hammocks for the night. This creature was a real horror, with a body six or seven inches in diameter and two great hooklike mandibles. Antu pinned it to a tree with a superb shot from his blowpipe. Its bite would have killed us instantly. It can leap ten yards in a single bound, and its web is so resistant and tough that even birds sometimes get caught in it: the spider sucks their blood.

That night, as I lay wrapped in my *chinchorro*, I found myself thinking about a certain episode in my past life; one particular man suddenly stirred in my memory. Women, opium, and whisky had begun to pall on me: I had sought refuge on a tiny island in the South China Sea, off the Gulf of Siam, whose entire population consisted of a brother and sister—twins—and their ancient, wrinkled old father. After seven months of this peaceful existence I woke up one morning to see a large lateen sail on the horizon: a Chinese junk. It was setting a course straight for the island, and those aboard must have been familiar with the place, because they steered unhesitatingly toward the one small landlocked anchorage. Finally they came about and dropped anchor. I hid in a thicket and watched. I saw some men come ashore with a body, which they proceeded to bury; then they took their casks over to a nearby spring and filled them with fresh water. I decided they were honest folk, and came out of hiding. The dead man turned out to have been their captain; now they were bound for Sarawak to take on a cargo of coconuts, destination Saigon. Unfortunately, none of them knew how to navigate. After my seven months' rest I was getting a little bored with this island, and the idea of visiting Sarawak and Saigon excited me. I told them I had once been a navigator, and said I was prepared to join them on their voyage. Even without this offer they were quite prepared to take me along as a supernumerary.

So I found myself in command of a Chinese junk, with a cut-price Indonesian crew. It was one of them who so resembled that giant spider: a huge, gross fellow, every inch of his body matted with hair, with buck teeth and bulging eyes and a square head, and vast hands capable of crushing any object they got hold of. Everyone was scared stiff of him, and I more than most. I was not quite twenty-three at the time. During the two months I stayed on board the junk I always managed to hold my own, but after certain scenes I witnessed, I used to lock myself in my cabin and sleep with my revolver under my pillow, within easy reach.

Of course, we were not bound for Sarawak at all, but to poach the offshore Dutch pearl fisheries, which lay uncomfortably within range of several coastal batteries. Our only equipment for this job consisted of the divers themselves, who went overboard at night with dark lanterns and sacks and brought back large quantities of oysters. One of them died from embolism, and another, who had a giant Cambodian as his diving partner, went down and never came up again. The Cambodian said a shark had got him, and nobody thought of questioning this explanation—not least since it meant one less for the share-out. Eventually we set a course for Saigon, where our junk dropped anchor in the delta, among countless others just like itself. A lean, dapper little man came aboard and bought all the pearls: I had to extract my share of the price at gun-point.

Next day, when the sun was at its zenith, we reached the near side of Diamond Mountain and went ashore at the point where Lolomai and I had had our private retreat—and where she now lay buried. The cross had fallen on its side in the long grass, and the hedge I had put up was indistinguishable from the rank surrounding undergrowth. I began to clear it with my machete. But what was the use? Any attempt to change the face of the jungle is so much labor lost. Even when I had done it successfully, as in the camp, what was the result?

This journey I had been so anxious to make with Antu now stood revealed for what it was: a valedictory gesture, the end of an era.

As though he had read my thoughts, Antu said: "Soon everything will be different here, too."

"Why? What do you mean?"

"Soon your people come here, too. They will kill the animals and fell the trees to build their huts. They will alter the course of the stream. The animals that escape being slaughtered will migrate southward—till they meet other men. And that will be the end of them. Our sons and our sons' sons will no longer rejoice in the game they still have available today. When the beasts of the jungle are no more, that will be the end of my people, too. More white men will come and take away our women. Oh, that has already happened once, long ago: it was then that the tribe migrated to its present home by the river. Old men told me this, who had it from other old men before them. Then you arrived, and your coming brought us no harm. But after you came others of your race;

and that was bad for us, very bad. Today what happened long ago will surely come to pass again."

I said nothing. There was nothing to say: Antu had spoken the truth. My journey here had not been originally prompted by any humanitarian motives. But afterward I had come to love the Taurepán and follow their way of life. I had honestly wanted to improve their conditions. And even if I had packed up and gone, the *racionales* would still have turned up in their hundreds, since Taurepán territory was rich in minerals and it was only surprising that the news had not got about sooner. Usually prospectors are intensely suspicious of anyone going off on his own, and never let one individual get the pickings in an area. First one group turns up, then another, and finally it turns into a stampede.

Antu made no further reference to the talk we had had by Lolomai's grave, and two days later we set off back to the village.

The first person we met on the return journey was Josephine: a stark-naked ebony statue, rounded and compact, hastening toward us with Marubu following close behind. The last time I had seen her there had been a note of bitterness in her voice, marked enough to make me wonder whether she was content with the life she had chosen. I reminded her of this.

"Oh no," she told me, "I'm really very happy. I'm mad about Marubu—it's extraordinary, we belong to different races, he can't speak my language and I'm having a job learning his, but I honestly think I couldn't live without him now. If it wasn't like that living out here would be impossible. But Marubu—why, it makes me feel good to look at him, right from the moment I wake up. It's good to work with him, too. But what scares me is any time we have to talk to another human being—he's jealous, you see, awful jealous, he never lets me come into camp with him. Suppose this setup closes down one day, what'll I do? What chance have I got of getting back to civilization again? Yes, I'm happy all right—but don't forget we exist, will you? Come and see us once in a while—"

She tumbled all this out in an incoherent jumble, nonstop.

While she was talking, a young vixen wandered up, eyes fixed on me. I remarked on its presence.

"Oh, she's mine," Josephine said. "Marubu killed her mother and so I brought her up, as a cub. She's built herself a burrow behind our hut, with two entrances. She's hungry now, it's her dinner-time."

The following day we arrived back in the village. Lay was a fully grown woman now, and Urulai showed herself most understanding about it. Preparations for the big hunting expedition were under way. They had already done some fishing, and their catch, cleaned and smoked and wrapped in palm leaves, now hung from the roof of the big central store hut.

Two diggers had levanted from the camp, and the Indians had refused to go out after them because they had a week's start. A jaguar had been at the chickens. Vaughan was flying in twice weekly to supply the *pulpero* with enough stores to last the winter. Mundo was furious because one of his wives had had another daughter. He cheered up when I told him about the kadyur. The fact that it had been a female was unimportant: the essential thing was that the animal itself still existed.

When I went around to the infirmary the doctor told me that he had cured two Indians of blennorrhea. One had three wives and the other two. Of the three wives one was old and ugly enough to run no risk of contamination by the diggers. I waited till the men of the village, with Mundo and Antu at their head, had gone off on their hunting expedition; then I sent for the three wives concerned. The doctor found that the oldest one was clean but the other two infected. That afternoon he had the remaining two wives around and discovered that they were both infected, too. This provided proof positive of the casual manner in which the Indian women were cuckolding their husbands, despite the sanctions they might incur. We were also able to identify the two carriers, a white man and a mulatto. That Saturday I sent them to the infirmary for treatment and made the following speech to the rest of the camp:

"The rainy season is almost due. We are going to have a long, idle, and extremely unpleasant winter. Before the weather breaks there's one hell of a lot you have to do. You must reinforce the roofs of your huts with an extra layer of palm leaves, and dig channels around them to drain the water off toward the river. You'll need to lay in a store of dry firewood, too: all that rain, as you'll find out, can make you extremely cold. And one more thing: leave the Indian women alone, or one fine day their husbands'll up and shoot the lot of you."

On his last freight trip Vaughan had asked me whether I wanted to fly out with him and spend the rainy season in Caracas. But I could not desert the Taurepán at this point.

I made a few repairs to the roof of our own hut, and laid in a pile of logs. I also had a rope strung from one bank of the river to the other, to ensure that people could get across even when the river was flooded, and carried out an inspection of all the huts in the village. It was rather like being aboard ship, I thought: we were taking on more fuel—logs, in this case—to arm ourselves against the storm ahead. And I recalled that as a young child I had been destined for a naval career—a commander, or better still an admiral, as my father used to say.

Well, it didn't turn out quite like that. My evening leap for freedom over the seminary wall eventually took me—after several hours' aimless wandering—to a railway station, as you will recall. At the platform stood a troop train bound for the front. I chucked my cassock into a patch of nettles, and under cover of darkness slipped unobserved aboard a truck carrying mules, as well as four or five soldiers. I hid myself in a heap of straw, where—being physically exhausted and emotionally wrung out—I proceeded to fall asleep. When I awoke it was day, but I dared not move. My throat was dry, and I could feel the blood pounding in my head. Finally the troop train ground to a halt; there was no sound of artillery, and I sensed that we were still well behind the front line. The soldiers got out and took the mules with them. By now I was feeling ravenous, and my hunger gave me the courage to come out of my hiding place. An N.C.O. spotted me and asked what the hell I was doing there. I had a sudden inspiration. "I want to get to the fighting," I said.

I was given some bread and a can of meat, I remember; then two policemen took me in charge, and a day or two later my father turned up to collect me. I had imagined all sorts of frightful reprisals, but in fact nothing like that happened at all. My father didn't give me a thrashing, or bawl me out; there was no question of my being punished. He put his arm around my shoulders, and rocked me gently to and fro as he talked. At first his words were nervous and abrupt, either because the situation was one he found embarrassing, or else on account of the great natural longing he must have felt to clasp me in his arms. Then, little by little, he began to speak calmly and persuasively, and everything he had to say was so right, so true, that I promised myself I would always comport myself as he would have wished, for the rest of my life.

My parents realized that a seminary was not, after all, the right place for me, and let me stay at home. In due course I reached my sixteenth birthday, and one day my father had a very serious talk with me. He had been observing me all this time, he said, and had come to the conclusion that what I was best suited to, by way of a career, was the Navy.

He arranged for me to attend a certain foreign naval training college, so that I might learn at least one other language fluently. I drank in his words with an enthusiasm that sped ahead of the detailed program he proceeded to unfold for my benefit, so that when he asked me if I agreed to the scheme, I said "Yes" without an instant's hesitation.

My first year at this training college was rather stiff going, but during the second year things went much better. Then there came a small incident which, nevertheless, was destined to have a decisive effect on the subsequent course of my life. During a Cadets' Ball the wife of one of my officers took a fancy to me, and shy though I was—after all, I was not yet eighteen, while she must have been over forty—in the end I went the whole hog with her. I used to visit her house regularly in the weeks that followed—till her husband came in and caught us, which put an abrupt end to my dream of becoming an admiral. I was expelled from the training college, and since I lacked the courage to show my face at home after such a *contretemps,* I shipped aboard a cargo vessel bound for Bangkok.

As I proceeded with my inspection of the village I mulled over these past episodes in my life, and came to the conclusion that—all things considered—I ought to be grateful to the romantic sparrow that stopped my chances of becoming a bishop, and the hot-blooded Captain's wife who had, similarly, blighted my prospects as a potential admiral.

The hunters were late in returning. The one tiny cloud that Antu had pointed out to me before their departure had now 'taken unto itself several others, much larger and more threatening. But the sun still shone brightly, and the sky was still, for the most part, clear and cloudless.

At last the distant barking of dogs could be heard. The women rushed out into the central square, while their children went scampering off to meet the hunters. Two or three of them came panting back, almost immediately, with news that broke on the village like a thunderclap: Mundo, the mighty chief, was dead.

Then the men arrived, dumped their game on the square without saying a word, and went off to bathe in the river. Antu and one other Indian were carrying the body, which lay on a rough litter of branches. They set it down beside the slaughtered animals; it was already in a state of putrefaction. Mundo, they told us, had died three days previously; he had been killed by an old boar, the leader of a herd. The boar itself was there too, its tusks still encrusted with Mundo's blood. It stood a good three feet at the shoulder, and had exceptionally sharp teeth. Its bristles were a yellowish gray; they resembled a porcupine's quills.

When Mundo had given the order to come down from the trees the herd had been in a decimated state, and the herd leader itself was lying on its side, badly wounded. But hardly had Mundo himself set foot on the ground when the old boar, rallying its last ounce of strength, got up and charged him. By the time the hunters finished the boar off Mundo was already done for. Man and beast died almost simultaneously.

Mundo's body was roped to the litter on which it had been brought in, and the litter itself was weighted with several large stones. A funeral procession formed up: coffin-bearers in front, then the witch doctor, wearing his full complement of amulets for the occasion, and finally the mourners, which meant the entire village. The witch doctor would intone melancholy phrases to which the crowd responded with wailing and lamentations. The litter was lowered into a deep river pool, and remained there for six days. Then the clean-picked skeleton was hauled up and left to dry in the sun. Later the bones were distributed among the various heads of families throughout the village. This was the highest possible mark of deference and affection, reserved for senior chiefs only.

Antu told me he had found another skeleton in the forest, picked clean by vultures: it probably was that of one of the fugitive diggers. The other escapee was picked up a day or so later by two natives, still alive, wandering up and down the forest in a hopeless attempt to reach the river. He was terribly emaciated, half dead on his feet. He had lost all his belongings, including his rifle and machete. All he had on him was an aluminum tube, of the sort used for packing Havana cigars, stuffed with diamonds.

By now the sky was almost completely overcast. The first intermittent lightning flashes grew in frequency and intensity, and the wind began to blow at gale force. Then the wind dropped, and the downpour began.

Chapter 16

◆

A SMALL CASE OF POACHING

Marubu turned up in camp a few days before the rainy season broke, and purchased large quantities of provisions. However fond he and Josephine were of each other, it looked like being a pretty cheerless winter for the poor girl, shut up in that isolated hut, her sole companions a half-wild vixen and a man she could exchange about half a dozen words with. Antu told me that Marubu had never dared confront the white men with a woman who was not of his own race; alone he could manage it, but the woman's presence would have exacerbated his sense of inferiority.

Very soon the diggers found themselves enjoying a compulsory holiday. They slept late, played interminable games of cards, listened to the radio, danced, and got drunk—the women more often than the men. And when they were drunk, they became quarrelsome. The women in their cups tended to display the one characteristic they had learned from the natives—lack of sexual inhibitions. They would call a man out from the store and have him there and then, very often in the pouring rain.

Days turned into weeks, a gray, monotonous sequence. The humidity of the atmosphere impregnated everything. The men saw their summer stores dwindling, and this made them uneasy. The least thing was liable to spark off a quarrel. I had built a large lockup, but I was obliged to divide it into four separate cells to prevent the occupants from massacring each other. A frequent source of disturbance was Marie-Pierre, the offspring of a French father and an Italian mother, who had been born in France and reached our camp by way of a brothel in Ciudad Bolívar. She had, somewhat unenthusiastically, shacked up with a digger who subsequently went sick. She had huge black eyes, a wide, generous mouth, prominent breasts, and considerable crude sex appeal, especially when she danced. She was, of course, well aware of the fact.

I sent for her one day and did my best to put on a stern expression.

"Look," I said, "you're an intelligent girl. You must realize I know all about your carryings-on in the camp. Aren't you ashamed of yourself? You've got a man of your own race who's ill, poor fellow—and the moment he's off to the infirmary you start taking on all comers, white, black, or mestizo! I don't care what you do personally, but I draw the line at a public scandal. You'd better be a bit more discreet in future, or I'll be forced to take some measures I guarantee you won't like one little bit."

"Señor, I don't go after these men—they come after me. Sure, I like them. I like them a lot. They can't resist me, and I can't resist them. I've always been that way, ever since I was a kid. I took up this life the first chance I got."

While she was talking I studied her: a sort of amorous cat with a French accent. Fetching. Very.

"Haven't you ever been in love?" I asked her.

"Oh yes: all my life."

"Listen," I said, "get this into your head once and for all: I don't want any trouble here. The next time you step out of line, I'm going to have you locked up in a hut across in the village, and kept there till the plane arrives."

"That would be a pleasure—provided you came to visit me now and then."

Making a great effort to control myself, I ruffled her hair and told her to clear off. At this moment, luckily, Tommasino came in. Subsequently Marie-Pierre was responsible for my getting myself involved in one of the most idiotic and embarrassing situations I have ever been in on account of a woman.

Everything was quiet in the village. The Indians had no savings to spend, since they squandered every last cent the minute they got it. I had opened a sort of credit bank in the store for the most willing workers, and there were also those natives with a permanent job, who earned regular wages all through the winter. Since the old principle of communal ownership still operated among them, they never went short of anything.

Antu had not yet been officially inducted as headman by the elders, since the moon had been on the wane after Mundo's death; but he ruled the tribe *de facto* and all obeyed him. He had found out about the wives who contracted blennorrhea, but took no steps to punish them. Mundo would not have hesitated for a moment.

For me personally this winter was very different from that first one, when Urulai and Lolomai would sally forth to find something better to offer me than the usual hunk of decaying meat that formed the tribe's staple diet. Now the fire blazed cheerfully day and night, and Lay and Urulai regarded themselves as the "great white chief's wives," a position that won them considerable respect. We even had a primitive shower, though Lay and Urulai always preferred to conform to the practice of the other village women, which meant waiting till the rain was really heavy and then marching out of the front door stark-naked.

I visited the camp only if there was some urgent decision that required my presence there, and every time I would see Marie-Pierre. She used to stand outside the door and grin at me. Her conduct, I was told, had taken a turn for the better: she paid frequent visits to her man in the infirmary, and no longer looked quite so like a cat in heat.

Pop, who had been steadily at work all this while, was convinced that the Rio Blanco had originally been a tributary of the Uai-parú: he had found the old stream bed, he told us. After taking numerous test borings, he and Tommasino between them had isolated several diamond-bearing seams. At this point the distance between the two rivers was about four hundred yards, and the difference in level some twenty-four feet—more than sufficient for us to divert the Rio Blanco into its former channel, thus exposing a considerable fresh stretch of the present bottom. This was probably rich in diamonds and, once drained, could continue to be sieved and washed throughout the winter.

I perceived, however, that the diversionary canal we would dig must inevitably strike the Rio Blanco just below a thirty-foot waterfall, and debouch into the deep pool that formed beneath it. The waterfall marked the boundary of my first concession, while the pool itself was outside it. I was afraid that, once the new channel had been opened, the mass of water in the pool might burst out, with catastrophic results. Pop and Tommasino assured me I had no need to worry on this score, and I authorized them to begin the operation. The diggers were working on commission, and therefore had an inducement to keep at it even during the heaviest downpour. They all agreed to turn out; and while the rain sluiced down on them they shoveled away, grumbling, stripped to the buff, but basically satisfied. The seam was not too deep down, and the undergrowth above it young and scanty. The proceeds would be divided equally after the Company had taken its percentage.

The Indians asked if they could join in the digging, and it was impossible to refuse them. The gangs left camp about midmorning and worked for not more than four or five hours. One day as I was in a canoe, on my way back to the village from the excavation site, I saw another canoe skimming downstream. Its occupant was Marubu, and he was paddling for dear life, the rain beating down on his naked torso. He appeared to be on his own, but when he reached the landing stage we saw Josephine lying in the bottom of the canoe. She looked like a corpse, but was still breathing. We carried her to the infirmary, and I sat by her bedside till, without regaining consciousness, she died. She was expecting a child, and had contracted pneumonia.

We buried her the next day, in a heavy downpour. Everyone was there at the graveside. Marie-Pierre, sublimely indifferent to the rest of us, prayed with noisy fervor. Marubu, who was next to me, stood like a stone, gazing blindly at the fresh mound of earth: he was still there when the rest of us had gone. That was the last we saw of him: from that day forth he vanished, and no one ever heard of him again.

At last, just as our stores were becoming dangerously depleted, the rains stopped. A south wind got up and blew the heavy clouds away; the sky became clear and blue once more, and the sun shone brightly. The villagers brought all their belongings out into the central square to air them, and the domestic animals luxuriated in the warmth. Maria, the storekeeper's woman, had a son—the first white baby to be born on the Uai-parú—and the *pulpero* handed out free meals and drinks all round. The prospectors had not stuck at their excavating long enough to complete the canal; they preferred to go back to their usual routine. The link between the Rio Blanco and the Uai-parú was eventually carried through with Indian labor.

One day Antu and I made a trip out to Josephine's old hut. We found the skeleton of the little vixen (she had probably died of terror and starvation), a few clothes, and, in a leather pouch, some ten small diamonds, together with one large blue one, a superb stone. Marie-Pierre's boy-friend was better again now, and I told Pop to assign him to Marubu's old claim: it was the one farthest from the camp. I was thinking rather too much about Marie-Pierre these days, and hoped in this way to get her off my mind. I had met her out in the forest once, and found myself unable to resist her. But I didn't want to become further involved.

Next morning the whole tribe was seething with activity: preparations had to be made for Antu's official induction ceremony. One group of men went off hunting, another to catch fish, while the women and children collected grubs and fruit or brewed *cachire*. I had a shrewd idea that Vaughan would probably roll up in time for the party, with a fresh load of provisions: the store was half empty.

Later in the afternoon I went across to the camp. The diggers had all gone off early, as Tommasino informed me.

Marie-Pierre had not, however, been able to leave camp with her lover; it appeared that of late she had not been feeling at all well, and was now in the infirmary. I felt I ought to check up on this personally. The doctor informed me that Marie-Pierre was suffering from acute nervous exhaustion. I followed him into his office, which was next door to the ward, and while he was making me some coffee I looked in on the patient.

"*Enfin!*" Marie-Pierre exclaimed. She gave me a long, searching look before she said anything else. "I thought I'd die," she told me. "You wanted to send me out there to end up the same way as Josephine. You don't want to have anything more to do with me, do you?"

I went out without saying anything. That night I slept badly —the first time such a thing had happened to me since taking on little Lay.

The feast to celebrate Antu's installation as chief was an exceptional one, and will certainly go down to posterity among the Taurepán. The entire population, myself included, put on the traditional costume—a palm-leaf skirt gathered around the waist with a thin length of liana. Antu also wore a head-piece of the same material, and sat enthroned on a big tree trunk full of fermenting *cachire*. Intoning paeans of praise to the moon, the Sapulí solemnly consecrated him chief of all the Taurepán. Mundo's deeds, together with those of other earlier leaders, were then recalled, after which the feasting and dancing began, a gluttonous orgy that lasted till dawn.

Marie-Pierre had begged me to let her join in the fun, but this was quite out of the question. She was back in circulation now, apparently quite well, and I made love to her again, this time in her hut. At the moment she must be there across the river with the rest of them, I thought, trying to spy out what was going on in the village. I watched the Indians, men and women alike, gradually working themselves up as they danced, and then having each other brutishly on the edge of the dancing floor or down by the river. I thought about Marie-Pierre. Nevertheless, I retired early, and so did my wives.

At the weekend the diggers streamed back to camp, Marie-

Pierre's fellow among them. Marie-Pierre herself promptly went sick again, and retired to the infirmary: she had obviously bewitched the doctor, too. During our last session she had told me that she no longer intended to go on living with this man, and had begged me to send him packing. She said he was violent and had sworn to kill her rather than lose her; but enamored as I was of Marie-Pierre, I was not prepared to let passion override both self-respect and common sense. The poor digger had only just recovered from a lengthy illness, and all his savings had been gobbled up by Marie-Pierre. Now he was beginning to earn again, and I felt it would be rank injustice to dismiss him at this stage. I seriously considered expelling Marie-Pierre, instead.

Saturday and Sunday passed in the normal way. Marie-Pierre played the malingerer in the infirmary, and her fellow hung around her till it was time for him to return to work. The moment he was gone, she returned to her hut. Now was my chance. I went across to the camp, having made up my mind to bring her back with me. I found her outside the door of her hut, as usual. She smiled at me. There were people around, and I beckoned her to follow me into the forest. I waited for her there, and when she saw me, she ran full tilt into my arms. I took her into a bamboo thicket and fell upon her as I had done twice before, but this time with even greater zest and fury.

Once again she had triumphed. As a member of the tribe I was entitled to four wives. I mentioned the matter to Antu, and found him agreeable. "If you want her you can have her," he said. "But she must respect our tribal laws." Even the witch doctor raised no objections. Lay was quite happy too: another marriage meant another feast. The only one to suffer was Urulai, but she had long been conscious that something had gone out of our relationship. I built another room onto our hut, and as soon as everything was ready Marie-Pierre crossed the river and entered tribal life. When her fellow returned to camp I had a talk with him. He told me I had got a lousy bargain, adding that the bitch would soon tire of me, too.

Life in the hut continued much as usual. Lay and Urulai

moved out into the new room, and Marie-Pierre now shared my big bed, with its tapir-skin coverlet. According to tribal law Urulai was mistress of the house, and Lay and Marie-Pierre were obliged to obey her; but Urulai was a kindly, amiable soul, who never gave orders. Marie-Pierre used to collect firewood, draw water from the river, and do the housework while Lay and Urulai were out gathering fruit. She taught Urulai a great deal; little by little the native girl conquered her shyness, and the two of them became good friends. Marie-Pierre learned a few words of Taurepán, and also got into the habit of bathing naked down at the river, in the company of equally naked men. All of them looked at her, nevertheless, rather differently from the way they regarded their other women: the witch doctor in particular seemed mesmerized by her charms. But none of them would have dared to lay a finger on her, and she knew it.

Urulai remained as gentle and good to me as ever; but despite her efforts to appear cheerful, I could see deep melancholy in her eyes, and this made me unhappy and guilty. One evening I went over to sleep with Urulai in the far room. She was crying. She embraced me tenderly, and all the time I was holding and caressing her she continued to sob under her breath. Next morning no sooner were Lay and Urulai out of the house than Marie-Pierre sprang on me like a tiger. "I don't care what Indian women do," she screamed. "*I'm* not a native, d'you hear? If you do that once more—just once—I swear I'll kill you!" It had, in fact, required conscious effort on my part to get any pleasure from sleeping with Urulai.

At long last Vaughan flew in with the first cargo of the new year, and various items of news, some of them unpleasant. Apparently a great many people were on their way to us, on foot or traveling by canoe; while others, in their anxiety to get here first, had started from British Guiana or Brazil.

The real bombshell burst a few days later.

The two Indians I had appointed our full-time hunters came and informed me that they had seen about thirty men digging in an area within the boundaries of my Number Five concession. This was the beginning of the end as far as my undisputed monopoly along the Uai-parú was concerned. I had been expecting it, of course, but troubles always turn up sooner than you think. The Indians had seen smoke, and thought it might indicate a forest fire. Instead, on investigation they had found about ten huts and thirty or so men, who were digging out a seam and carting the shale down to the river to wash it.

I at once informed Antu, and we agreed they had to be driven out. Our plan was as follows. Antu was to set off through the forest with thirty of his own men, while I traveled by river, taking ten canoes, four men in each. We would keep going throughout the night and the following day. That night we would establish contact between the two groups by means of the owl signal, and together we would raid the encampment at dawn. We made quite sure everyone knew exactly what he had to do—who was standing guard, who had to disarm the men, whose job it was to search the huts.

My group set out some while before Antu's, since the journey was a longer one by river. While we glided along I found myself thinking back over my past life. I had won quite a few battles, and lost almost as many. When I first reached the Uai-parú I had been ragged, hungry, at the end of my tether. Was this to be another lost battle? The thirty who had turned up in pursuit of a fortune were an advance guard only: soon people would be arriving in their thousands. If word got around that these pioneers had been murdered by savages, would that stop the rest of them? Not a hope: the most it could achieve was a delay of a few months—a year, perhaps—before the main phalanx moved in. Whatever happened, the rush was on: it was not only my concessions that contained gold and diamonds, but the entire belt south of the Fifth Parallel, as far as the headwaters of the Amazon. Who could hope to hold up this tidal wave of cupidity?

And in its wake would come traders and merchants, diamond traffickers, law and order. The great robber barons who flourished in the nineteenth century might not have hesitated to eject this first group of bum prospectors if they threatened to ruin their own well-ordered schemes; but I had been born in a later age, and at Bertinoro, the very home of good living and hospitality, which lies between Forlimpopoli and fair Cesena. When I was a boy in Bertinoro, I had once gone off with a friend to look for Barbarossa's treasure in the caves beneath the Castello. We got lost, and couldn't find our way out again. Eventually we were rescued, more dead than alive, and very lucky not to have been eaten by the giant rats that breed down there.

At first light Antu gave the signal: three short calls. Silent as ghosts, the Indians surrounded the huts; and five minutes later some thirty rifles, machetes, and sheath knives lay in a heap on the ground. The men, still half asleep, lined up outside, and Antu's Indians stood covering them with drawn bows.

"Who's your leader?" I asked.

All eyes turned in the direction of a tall, lean individual, who came slouching across to me, unrecognizable at first in the dim light of dawn, but then revealing himself as the Hungarian I had previously expelled from the camp.

"How long have you been here?" I asked him.

"About ten days."

"Didn't you realize you were on my claim?"

"No."

"You must have crossed the boundary line. It's clearly marked; you couldn't miss it."

"We never thought any claims would extend this far. We didn't know—"

"All right, all right," I said. "Let it go. Just let's be having your diamonds."

The man hesitated.

"Come on," I said. "You know perfectly well I'll find them in the long run."

The Hungarian vanished into his hut and came back with one of those round cigarette tins. It was almost full.

"Nice work," I said, and shoved it into my pocket.

"You can't take them all!" he exclaimed.

"True. I propose to sort and value them, and then give you fifty per cent. That's the rule—as you well know."

The Hungarian seemed reassured by this. "Could we have the equivalent in provisions?" he inquired.

"Yes, if you prefer it. See you in camp, then."

Before we left the area I had Antu's men set fire to the huts. The Hungarian informed me that other free-lance prospectors must by now have arrived in the neighborhood.

Out of those thirty men—a mixed bunch of Europeans, Negroes, and half-castes—not one wanted to stay on the concession, apart from two who were ill, and these we transported to the infirmary. The rest, loaded down with provisions, made off in a southwesterly direction, hacking their way through the jungle. They built a fresh camp about seven miles away, in an open glade by one of the Uai-parú's tributaries. Here they struck both diamonds and gold. Very soon they had leveled out a small airstrip, and in next to no time there were a hundred free-lance prospectors in the area. Some of the men working on the concessions went over to them. As I had foreseen, at least a sprinkling of diamonds cropped up everywhere. The storekeeper found himself swamped with competitors. Other pilots arrived in Vaughan's wake. Diamond buyers multiplied. Finally—and inevitably—the Guardia Nacional turned up, to enforce governmental law and order. The rule of the strongest was at an end.

Chapter 17

♦

ANTU'S FAREWELL

The Indians working to divert the course of the Rio Blanco had come to the end of their job. A day came when the first thin thread of water ran trickling along the channel we had dug, and very soon the gap began to widen. Then the earthen rampart that was still holding back the water from the pool collapsed, and a great tidal wave came crashing through. The level dropped twenty-four feet in four hundred yards; there was no force on earth that could have held up those countless tons of water. The wave whirled earth and tall trees before it in its tumultuous passage; the pool was left practically empty; and the Rio Blanco had a new course.

The Indians test-dug the seam in the pool and turned up gold and diamonds in abundance. But the pool lay outside my concession, and the boundary marks were all too visible. The news spread through the forest like wildfire. Soon the first free-lance prospectors were on the scene. Huts sprouted in fungoid profusion. In the first three weeks there were eight deaths from accidents or fights. The diggers made a packet, got drunk, and went off after the Indian women. More than once I was forced to intervene. But I could not prevent more than one prospector's vanishing in the forest and never being seen again.

Finally a detachment of the Guardia Nacional showed up, with a sergeant in command. His first authoritative act was to prohibit the sale of liquor; but in a very few days you could get a drink again as easily as ever—except that now it cost rather more. The sergeant came around to see me and said he had looked up the law relating to concessions; while a claim was private property for the purpose of mining it, and extracting gold and diamonds from its soil, the owner (meaning me) could not forbid free passage through the area to anybody. I tried to make him see that a battle royal could start up at any time between the Indians and the diggers, bearing in mind the overbearing insolence of the one party and the natural bitterness and distrust felt by the other. I begged him at least to keep the village out of bounds. He replied that this was quite impossible: all Venezuelan soil was open to any Venezuelan citizen who chose to march over it. He added that he was only awaiting authorization from the capital before undertaking a levy for military service, and that one of the first to be called up would be none other than Antu.

The sergeant was a mulatto and had no great love for the Indians. Indeed, he actively enjoyed tormenting them, and made their lives plain hell in a number of most ingenious ways.

As though I had not got enough to contend with just now, Marie-Pierre was always making fresh trouble for me. She had become a complete domestic tyrant, doing nothing herself, ordering Lay and Urulai about and making them wait on her, and in general behaving like a spoiled lady of the manor. She was also making a spirited attempt to bewitch the witch doctor, and even ogled the mulatto sergeant on occasion. In fact, she was a whore by temperament, with just the right vital statistics to make the job pay. Naturally, her version of events was quite different: the medicine man was molesting her, and the sergeant was pestering her to marry him. My first fine careless rapture had by now evaporated: Marie-Pierre was a bore. I disliked the tone of voice she used with Urulai, and once come back to my senses I realized that the native girl was worth ten of her. One day I caught her screaming at Lay, in a manner that I detested. Abruptly I knew that it was all over between me and Marie-Pierre. So I made arrangements with Antu and Vaughan, and one day we carried

her down to the plane, dumped her in a seat, and strapped
her up. Before leaving, I dropped a sealed envelope in her
lap.

With Marie-Pierre's departure peace was restored to the
medicine man and Urulai regained her old serenity. (Lay had
no such problems: she found life continually enjoyable, both
by age and by temperament.) But for the village in general
there was no return of the old peaceful ways. One Indian,
who had become a chronic drunk, but could no longer get
hold of any liquor, offered his own wives in exchange for a
bottle of rum. Despite my protests, the sergeant let this deal
go through. Later I found out that a clandestine still had
been set up in the forest under his "protection." The women
were scared half out of their wits, and everyone was afraid
something really awful might happen at any moment. Perhaps
the sergeant was hoping for just such an incident: it would
justify his taking stronger measures against the Indians. Antu
knew I was on his side, but he also realized that there was
little one could do against a band of armed and permanently
intoxicated scoundrels.

Then one day the serious incident happened.

The newcomers had discovered the other village to the
south of us, which was inhabited by a few families who were
growing yuca. Five freebooting diggers went off there one
day in a canoe, taking with them several bottles of the filthy
illicit liquor from the still. They never came back. One of the
villagers arrived that same evening to tell Antu what had
happened.

The diggers had been drunk by the time they got there,
and offered drinks all around to the men of the tribe. No
one had accepted. Then the diggers began clamoring for
women. The old headman, Lay's father, had prudently hidden
them all away in the jungle. The drunks found one old crone
sick in bed, and hurled themselves on her. When her husband
tried to defend her he had his thigh slashed open with a
machete. His scream of pain acted on the rest of the villagers
like a starter's gun. From every direction men came running,
and in a few moments the five diggers were dead.

We took the messenger back with us, and reached the village in two hours. No one had as yet touched the bodies. The old man who had been slashed had died from loss of blood. The women were back from their forest hide-out, weeping over the old man. The men wandered around between the wailing women and the corpses, looking furtively pleased with themselves: they moved with an air of conscious pride.

I tried to explain to Antu what the sergeant's reaction would be when he found out about this. I also did what I could to enlighten Lay's father. The law of the *racionales* is inexorable, I told them. A life for a life. I pounded my fist by way of emphasis.

Finally, when I had got them thoroughly scared, I decided to risk it. The five dead men were loaded into the same canoe with which they had arrived in the village. We hauled it some way downstream, dumped the bodies into a deep pool, and chucked their bottles and machetes in after them. Then we overturned the canoe and let it drift away with the current, keel uppermost. The dead Indian was buried in his hut, and the hut itself then set on fire. Every trace of blood was removed. I told them not to say a word to anyone about the incident, and to be extremely polite and helpful if the sergeant came asking them questions.

Antu and I were back in the main village by the time dawn broke.

Late that same evening, when I had already retired for the night, Antu came around to my hut and asked me to take a walk with him. The moon was high in the heavens, and its radiance shone on the deserted village square. We sat down on the riverbank, side by side.

"I have made up my mind," Antu said. "I am going to leave this district."

I remembered how one morning in Caracas he had told me of his decision to go back to the Uai-parú. It was in the same tone of voice that he made this new announcement.

"What do you mean?" I asked.

"I want to go away from here. I feel I must take my people

away from here. We shall return to our old way of life—
hunting, fishing, gathering fruit. I shall try to make them
forget money, and all the things that we have, through force
of circumstance, learned from you, the white man. My tribe
will be happy only when it is far away from all white men."

I realized that nothing in the world would ever make him
change his mind. By now I knew him as well as I knew
myself.

"Do I count for nothing?" I said.

"You are my brother, my father. You are like Mauri to me.
But not even you can do anything to save my people. Our
one hope lies in the forest."

There was a long silence. I was so stricken by grief that I
could not speak. Then Antu, in a voice I shall never forget,
cried: "*Marusa ka—marusa ka*—Why did you ever come here?"

"Where will you go?"

Antu raised one arm and pointed to the south.

"We will set as great a distance between ourselves and
your people as we can, so that our children may be able to
grow up and die in peace." He paused, then added: "I shall
take Lay and Urulai with me."

"Yes, Antu: you are right, of course."

"I am glad I have spoken with you. I want to say this, too:
we wish you well, and we should be happy to have you
among us again, on the banks of another river where the fish
are plentiful, and in the heart of another rich forest such as
this, where you can have a fine new hut, as big as you want."

"True, Antu. But then I should become as you were in
Caracas. One fine morning I, too, would wake full of yearning
for my own people, and ready to die of misery and boredom."

When we got up and walked home the moon was sinking,
and I lay awake till sunrise.

Next afternoon the head of every family gathered before the
central hut, and heard Antu publicly pronounce his decision
—which he did after enumerating the many wrongs the tribe
had suffered without possible defense or redress.

All unanimously agreed that preparations for departure
should be begun at once. Antu advised them to bring only

the bare necessities of existence: bows, arrows, hunting knives, and machetes. He urged them to bring as much yuca as they could carry. When he rose to return to his hut, I dared not follow him. He was indeed the chief, and I remained seated, like all the rest, following him with my eyes.

I spent my last night with Urulai, full of tenderness and regret for all the suffering I had caused her. She said nothing; it was always hard to make Urulai talk. But she clung to me all night through, and would not sleep.

Before dawn broke the whole tribe was ready, including the families from the two outlying villages, who had come in the previous night. One by one, they said good-by to me, though beyond any doubt I was the reason for their abandoning the land and forest that they loved so well. Then Antu came forward, followed by two Indians who were carrying about ten carbines between them. They laid these weapons at my feet.

"They would soon be unserviceable," Antu said. "Why burden ourselves with useless luggage?" Then he looked straight at me and added: "If you had not come, it would have been someone else. It is not your fault. We shall continue to roam our forests as our fathers did before us."

The sun was just coming up when Antu gave the signal to move off. All of them, children included, carried great bundles of yuca on their backs. Antu marched at the head of the column, and slowly it wound away up that long hillside that the two of us had climbed together on our journey to civilization.

Siskuss did not want to leave me. I took off my belt and knotted one end of it about his neck. Then I ran along the column till I found Urulai, and gave the dog into her charge. Urulai was weeping, though Lay, next to her, had the cheerful air of someone just off to a party. Siskuss was a good dog; he would be much more use to them, on their journey, than to me.

I felt I must say some last word to Antu before the forest swallowed him forever. I called his name, and ran forward, trying to catch up with him. Someone heard me and passed

the word on. Antu stepped aside while the column continued
to move.

"Antu," I said, "I am leaving here too. I shall go back to
my own people. I cannot stay here without you. Somewhere
in this great forest you will find another river, as fine as this
one—perhaps better. But before you settle it, before you build
one single hut, make quite, quite sure that no diamonds lie
hidden there."

I stood and watched the procession pass on, till the last
Indian had vanished into the jungle, and the exodus was
accomplished. And still Antu's gentle, melancholy voice echoed
in my mind, saying, again and again: *"Marusa ka—marusa ka
—Why did you ever come here?"*